Traditional Mexican Style Interiors

Text by Donna McMenamin

Photography by Richard Loper

4880 Lower Valley Road, Atglen, PA 19310 USA

Dedication

To all the *maestros* who pour their hearts and souls into creating the architectural details and works of art that beautify our homes, and to the laborers who install them.

Library of Congress Cataloging-in-Publication Data

McMenamin, Donna.
  Traditional Mexican style interiors/text by Donna McMenamin; photography by Richard Loper.
    p. cm.
  ISBN 0-7643-1693-1 (hardcover)
1. Interior decoration--Mexico--Themes, motives.
I. Loper, Richard. II. Title.
  NK2014.A1 M35 2003
  747'.0972--dc21
                    2002010933

Designed by "Sue"
Type set in Impact/Korinna BT

ISBN: 0-7643-1693-1
Printed in China

Published by Schiffer Publishing Ltd.
4880 Lower Valley Road
Atglen, PA 19310
Phone: (610) 593-1777; Fax: (610) 593-2002
E-mail: Schifferbk@aol.com
Please visit our web site catalog at
www.schifferbooks.com
We are always looking for people to write books on new and related subjects. If you have an idea for a book, please contact us at the above address.

This book may be purchased from the publisher.
Include $3.95 for shipping. Please try your bookstore first.
You may write for a free catalog.

In Europe, Schiffer books are distributed by
Bushwood Books
6 Marksbury Ave. Kew Gardens
Surrey TW9 4JF England
Phone: 44 (0)20 8392-8585; Fax: 44 (0)20 8392-9876
E-mail: Bushwd@aol.com
Free postage in the UK. Europe: air mail at cost.
Please try your bookstore first.

Acknowledgements

A book such as this does not happen without a great deal of cooperation from old friends and acquaintances, and of course new *amigos* we made along the way. We would like to take this opportunity to thank them all. First and foremost, we wholeheartedly express our gratitude to all of the homeowners who relinquished their privacy and graciously gave us access to their personal domains. Not only did they graciously open their doors, but many had to do so in the early morning hours. (While a 6:30 am schedule might not seem too early for many of us in the States, for Mexico, it is unheard of.) Many of the homeowners fed us along the way and provided transportation, which made lugging our equipment much easier, and for that we are extremely appreciative. Our warmest thanks go to John & Nancy Alegret, Stan Avison & Bruce Ericksen, Craig Baugh, Thomas E. Black III, Tonia & Bob Clark, Carol & Roger Collier, Sande Deitch, Anna Franklin, Rhea & Leon Gary and their agent Mary Barbara Scott, Marc Gerson, Milagros & Rafael Ghinis, Ricardo González and Maria Ramírez, Nicholas Power & Penelope Haskew, Luis Felix Hernández & Dorothy Mann de Hernández, Janet & Fred Heyne and their staff, with a special thanks to Raul Briones, Rachel Horn, Richard Leet and his staff, Bill & Heidi LeVasseur and staff, John & Bettie Moser, Jorge & Maria Peña, Mary Ann & Ron Peterson, Sue Pittman and her staff, Bill Reiner & Stanton Gray, Terry & Jack Reinhart, Judith Richardson, Judith Roberts, Raye & Noble Robinson, Isidra Salazar Olmos, Dean & Filomena Saxton, Lynn & Dave Shaw, and Mike & Jayne Wachs. Additionally, there are those who wished to remain anonymous, and as much as we would like to acknowledge them here, we must respect their wishes, but a big thanks to them as well.

In San Miguel de Allende, we owe a huge thank you to Jennifer Hamilton, who single-handedly sought out some of the finest San Miguel *casas* for us to scout. She supplied us with an extraordinary amount of information regarding some sixty homes in San Miguel prior to our arrival and she continued her support throughout the entire trip. We could not have accomplished the San Miguel shoot without her, and we are absolutely indebted to her. *Muchas gracias*, Jennifer.

Several others gave their time, assistance, and encouragement along the way, including Suzy and Roberto Alvarado, Patti Behr, Dave Carter, Lou Christine, Nancy Dusseau, Clyde Ellis, Christopher & Caroline Fallon, Bonnie Gibson, Bob & Jennifer Haas, Alice Dale Kimsey, Barbara Kraus, Bonnie Kuykendall, Christy Martin, Jim Miegs, Barbara & Jeffrey Minker, Mary Mohr, Salvador Orozco, Jed Paradies, Debra Raeber, Rick & Marybeth Rosenthal, Ron Slaughter, Linda Solomon, Joel Stocker & Tom Brightman, Nancy Swickard, and Sondra Zell.

We truly appreciated the opportunity we had to photograph several pottery artists at work at *Majolica Santa Rosa taller*. Our thanks to the owner, Isidra Salazar Olmos, and to the artists: José Ramírez Martínez, Maria Cruz Aguilar González, Rosa Angélica Hernández, and Beatriz Angélica Jaramillo Villalobos.

Gracias to Karen Ramsey of Benjamin Moore & Company and to Joe Ingegneri, Tim Bosveld, and Jose Enriquez of Dunn-Edwards Corporation for supplying specific paint color sample cards.

Religious art experts and dealers, James Caswell (Santa Monica) and Martha Egan (Santa Fe), were consulted to identify *Santos* and *retablos*. In addition, when stumped as to the exact origin of an old California tile mural at Red Thunder Ranch, antique tile dealer, Scott Wells (Los Angeles) came to the rescue. We are grateful for knowledgeable friends.

We were both extremely pleased that architect Rafael Rios-Ghinis agreed to be interviewed, and provided explanations for those illusive architectural terms, like *ojo de buey*. As an architect from Mexico, now designing and residing in Tucson, his insights proved invaluable in understanding the Mexican home from both sides of the border.

Kudos to our editor and publisher, Nancy and Peter Schiffer, who never hesitated when approached about the concept of this book and have been supportive as always.

We should not forget that the beauty of these homes and their lush surroundings is founded upon the dreams and visions of architects and designers. Without this starting point, their drawing boards, none of these homes would have become a reality. These homes are works of art and will remain standing long after our time has passed.

And finally, a very special and affectionate thank-you to our spouses, David and Linda, who endured our absences from home and gave us the time and space necessary to complete this project.

Credits

Name of home: **La Casa que Abraza el Cielo** (The House that Embraces the Sky)
Year Built: 1998
Owner: Anonymous
City: Tucson, Arizona
Architect: Ron Robinette
Landscape: Richard Wogisch
Interior Decorator: Christy Martin of Studio Encanto
Builder: Mike Wachs of Mike Wachs Construction Company
Pages: 8, 35, 52, 93, 96, 108, 113, 134, 142, 146, 151, 153, 163, 171, 178, 179

Name of home: **Casa de Alegret**
Year Built: 1986—additions 1999
Owners: John and Nancy Alegret
City: Tucson, Arizona
Architects: David Goff (original home) David Wilson (additions)
Pages: 109, 156

Caption Designation: **Casa de Anonymous**
Owner: Anonymous
City: Houston, Texas
Pages: 24, 50, 67, 164, 165, 167, 169, 179

Caption Designation: **Casa de Baugh**
Owner: Craig Baugh
City: Tucson, Arizona
Page: 173

Caption Designation: **Casa de Black**
Owner: Thomas E. Black III
City: Tucson, Arizona
Landscape: Plants of Distinction
Pages: 28, 55, 178

Name of home: **Casa Chorro**
Year built: circa 1800, remodeled 1999
Owner: Richard Leet
City: San Miguel de Allende, Guanajuato, Mexico
Pages: Title page, 45, 46, 62, 69, 141, 160

Caption Designation: **Casa de Clark**
Year Built: 1997
Owners: Tonia and Bob Clark
City: Houston, Texas
Architect: Michael T. Landrum
Landscape Architect: Sarah W. Lake
Pages: 29, 48, 49

Name of home: **Casa de la Condessa** (House of the Contessa)
Year built: circa 1960, remodeled 2000
Owner: Sande Deitch
City: San Miguel de Allende, Guanajuato, Mexico
Architectural Designers: Caroline and Christopher Fallon (remodeling)
Landscape Designer: Alfonso Alarcón
Interior Decorator: Sande Deitch and Christopher Fallon
Pages: 12, 30, 31, 47, 60, 68, 70, 83, 107, 128, 129

Name of home: **Casa de la Cuesta** (House on the Hill) (Bed & Breakfast)
Year built: 1999
Owners: Bill and Heidi LeVasseur
City: San Miguel de Allende, Guanajuato, Mexico
Arquitecto: Francisco Molina
Pages: 19, 44, 74, 75, 101, 114, 136, 150, 161, 182

Caption Designation: **Casa de Franklin**
Owner: Anna Franklin
City: Tucson, Arizona
Pages: 58, 184

Caption Designation: **Casa de Ghinis**
Owners: Milagros and Rafael R. Ghinis
Year Built: 1930, addition: 1995
Arquitecto: Rafael-Rios Ghinis (addition)
City: Tucson, Arizona
Pages: 23, 33, 64, 153, 160, 175, 176

Name of home: **Casa Heyne**
Year Built: 2000
Owners: Janet and Fred Heyne
City: San Miguel de Allende, Guanajuato, Mexico
Arquitecto: Pedro Urquiza
Landscape Designer: Timeteo Wachter
Pages: 17, 18, 42, 43, 60, 61, 71, 72, 76, 78, 79, 81, 95, 97, 98, 102, 108, 116, 117-123, 141, 144, 145, 150, 152, 170

Name of home: **Casa Hidalgo**
Year built: circa 1780, remodeled 2000
Owner: Richard Leet
City: San Miguel de Allende, Guanajuato, Mexico
Interior Decorator: Rachel Horn
Pages: 29, 38, 57, 59, 85, 92

Name of home: **Casa Kino**
Year Built: 1998
Owner: Marc Gerson
City: Tucson, Arizona
Architect: John Gabb and Marc Gerson, Architectural Designer
Landscape: Marc Gerson and Plants of Distinction
Interior Decorator: Marc Gerson of Marc New West Design, Inc.
Pages: 56, 63, 94

Name of home: **La Casa Lomita Linda** (The Pretty Little Hill House)
Year Built: 1985, remodeled 2000
Owners: Roger and Carol Collier
City: Tucson, Arizona
Architect: David Shambach and James Meigs, architectural designer (remodeling)
Landscape: Dan Elder
Interior Decorator: Diane Love
Pages: 15, 24, 25, 37, 56, 65, 86, 89, 95, 98, 110, 124-126, 143, 158, 161, 174, 177

Caption Designation: **Casa de Moser**
Owners: John and Bettie Moser
Year Built: 1990
City: Tucson, Arizona
Architectural Designer: Mike and Jayne Wachs of Mike Wachs Construction Company
Pages: 27, 40, 68, 86, 92, 105, 135, 147, 151-153, 162

Name of home: **Casa del Parque** (House in the Park)
Year built: 1995
Owners: Ricardo González and Maria Ramírez
City: San Miguel de Allende, Guanajuato, Mexico
Arquitecto: Manuel Barbosa
Landscape: José Bautista
Page: 104

Name of home: **Casa de los Perros** (House of the Dogs)
Year built: unknown, remodeled 2001
Owner: Sue R. Pittman
City: San Miguel de Allende, Guanajuato, Mexico
Architectural Designer: Christopher Fallon (remodeling)
Interior Decorator: Sue R. Pittman
Pages: 19, 38, 132, 157, 159, 183

Name of home: **Casa Poco a Poco** (House Little by Little)
Year built: 1991
Owners: Jorge and Maria Eugenia Peña
City: San Miguel de Allende, Guanajuato, Mexico
Page: 159

Caption Designation: **Casa de Reinhart**
Year built: circa 1960, remodeled 1995
Owners: Jack Reinhart and Therese Kutt Reinhart
City: San Miguel de Allende, Guanajuato, Mexico
Arquitecto: Juan Carlos Valdés A. (remodeling)
Pages: 20, 101

Caption Designation: **Casa de Roberts**
Year built: 1970
Owner: Judith Roberts
City: San Miguel de Allende, Guanajuato, Mexico
Architectural Designer: Francisco Garcia Valencia
Pages: 28, 39, 100, 134, 162, 168

Caption Designation: **Casa de Robinson**
Owners: Raye and Noble Robinson
Year Built: 1999
City: Tucson, Arizona
Architect: Matthew Hamilton
Builder: Michael Nicholas
Landscape: Harlows
Interior Decorator: Owner, Virginia Manzer, and Sharmin Pool-Bok
Pages: 33, 63, 90, 99, 111, 163

Name of home: **Casa del Sol y Luna** (House of the Sun & Moon)
Year Built: 2000
Owners: Donna and David McMenamin
City: Tucson, Arizona
Arquitecto: Rafael Rios-Ghinis
Pages: 21, 22, 36, 50, 66, 73, 80, 87, 93, 103, 115, 116, 127, 128, 154, 156, 170-172 175, 180, 181

Caption Designation: **Casa de Wachs**
Owners: Michael and Jayne Wachs
Year Built: 1995
City: Tucson, Arizona
Architectural Designer: Mike and Jayne Wachs of Mike Wachs Construction Company
Interior Decorator: Jayne Wachs
Pages: 14, 26, 34, 47, 51, 64, 77, 91, 106, 112, 137, 138, 140, 149, 151, 182, 185

Name of home: **El Castillo** (The Castle)
Year Built: 1932, outdoor *sala* added 1999
Owners: Mary Ann and Ron Peterson
City: Tucson, Arizona
Architect: Josias Joesler (original) and Alexandra Hayes (addition)
Pages: 54, 148, 155

Name of home: **Estrella de la Mañana** (Morning Star)
Year built: circa 1690s, remodeled 1996 into existing walls
Owners: Rhea and Leon Gary
City: San Miguel de Allende, Guanajuato, Mexico
Architect: Hal Box (remodeling)
Landscape: Joseph Turner
Interior Decorator: Marsha Brown and owner
Pages: 13, 16, 40, 41, 82, 84, 130, 131, 139, 144, 146, 166

Name of home: **La Flor del Desierto** (The Flower of the Desert)
Year Built: 1998, guest-house added 2001
Owners: Dave Shaw and Lynn Mitchener Shaw
City: Tucson, Arizona
Architectural Designer: James Meigs
Cantera Master: Don Lupe Garcia
Wood Master: Salvador Orozco
Pages: 32, 53, 88, 92, 102, 152, 176, 180

Name of home: **Red Thunder Ranch**
Year Built: 1922, remodeled 1996
Owners: Stan Avison and Bruce Ericksen
City: Corona de Tucson, Arizona
Architect: Bob Taylor (remodeling)
Pages: 16, 27, 57, 62, 67, 69, 74, 111, 133

Name of home: **Villa Scorpio al Puente** (Villa of the Scorpion by the Bridge) (Bed & Breakfast)
Year built: circa 1730s, remodeling on-going
Owners: Nicholas Power and Penelope Haskew
City: San Miguel de Allende, Guanajuato, Mexico
Pages: 98, 130

Author's Preface

After the release of *Popular Arts of Mexico 1850-1950*, I was asked the same question over and over—How did you get the idea for the book, get it started, etc.? It appears that readers are quite interested in these facts, so with that in mind, allow me to explain how *Traditional Mexican Style: Interiors* and *Traditional Mexican Style: Exteriors* came to be.

With construction completed on *Casa del Sol y Luna*, I embarked on another trip to Mexico with my longtime shopping companion, Marilyn, in order to buy appropriate finishing accessories. As our trip was drawing to a close, our friend Jorge, wanted to show us his home and surrounding neighborhood. We only had a few minutes, as we were enroute to the airport, but in that brief period, what I saw made a profound impact on me—the architecture, its details, and the colors of the *casas* were incredibly beautiful! I turned to Marilyn and made the statement "there is a book in here somewhere."

I guess with that small declaration, I planted a seed somewhere in my subconscious because I could not seem to shake the idea, no matter how hard I tried— and I did try. I really did not want to take on the task of another book, especially one where I did not have any sources. At least in *Popular Arts*, I knew where collections resided and those would become that book's foundation, but for this project, I had no starting point. How would I find the homes, and once I did, would I be able to persuade the owners to let me in for a peek? Would they subsequently grant permission for photography? Those details worried me, but I put them aside for the moment.

I presented the book idea to my husband, David. I wanted his opinion on the concept and his reaction to me taking on another project of this magnitude. He thought it was a good idea and I was out of the starting blocks, so to speak, but just ahead of me, several hurdles required clearance.

Richard Loper, the photographer from *Popular Arts*, was the first hurdle—would he be interested in becoming a partner in this endeavor? Fortunately, he was very enthusiastic and agreed to the project without much hesitation. Next up, could I persuade Rafael Rios-Ghinis, a Mexican architect, to agree to an interview and provide technical support as needed? *Si*. Two hurdles safely maneuvered and another one approaching. What would Schiffer Publishing think of the concept and would they agree to publish it? Again, there was enthusiasm. Now, with a willing partner/photographer, a Mexican architect, and a publisher, I was definitely in the race.

Looming down the track were huge hurdles—finding appropriate homes and subsequently gaining access and permissions. I began in my own back yard—Tucson, (a.k.a., the Old Pueblo). The Spanish settled Tucson in 1776 and Mexico controlled the city from 1821 until the Gadsden Purchase of 1854. Four mountain ranges—Santa Catalinas, Santa Ritas, Rincons and the Tucson Mountains—surround this beautiful city that sits in the saguaro-studded Sonoran desert. It is no surprise that the Old Pueblo lends itself to Mexican architecture: (1) the topography is similar to Mexico, (2) there is a long Spanish history, (3) the close proximity to the Mexican border (about sixty miles), and (4) Tucson averages three hundred sixty days of sunshine per year. As with Mexico, outdoor living is a way of life here and the homes are designed to capitalize on that fact along with the incredible mountain and desert vistas. After several months of scouting, the Tucson shoot became a reality and includes homes built as early as 1902 and as late as 2000.

With the Tucson photography completed, it was time to focus on San Miguel de Allende, a city with incredible architecture located one hundred eighty miles northwest of Mexico City, in the state of Guanajuato. Founded in 1542, it is a Spanish Colonial jewel that has become one of Mexico's protected National Monuments. Because of that fact, any new construction in the historic district must conform to the colonial style, complete with a strict set of architectural guidelines. Keeping that in mind, it might prove difficult to ascertain the age of the *casas* presented here, without peeking at the Credits page, as we illustrate homes built from the 18th century to the present.

I chose to organize both of these books by category, as this method has proved itself invaluable to decorators, architects, builders and homeowners. For example, if you are looking for kitchen ideas and inspiration, it is a simple matter to peruse the chapter on *cocinas* in *Traditional Mexican Style: Interiors*. In addition, if you want to view one house in its entirety, please refer to the Credits of both books.

An important aspect of the Mexican home is color, and I decided early into the project to try to include the name and manufacturer of paint colors we encountered along the way, whenever possible. Unfortunately, this was not feasible for the homes photographed in San Miguel, because, in all cases, the painters mix the colors on-site with several different powdered pigments and a lime-wash known as *cal*. However, with the Tucson homes, we were more fortunate. You will find the paint color name in the caption, and further information in the *Paint Sample Illustrations* in Appendix 2.

Aside from paint, there is one particular *talavera* tile (*medio-pañuelo*) that we found installed quite frequently in these homes. It is one of the most versatile tile designs ever produced, due to its color variety and installation patterns. Therefore, I felt it might be beneficial to provide an illustration as further clarification (see Appendix 1).

I believe that you will discover that traditional Mexican homes are some of the most beautiful, warm and inviting homes ever designed. Nothing can quite compare with their architectural lines and details, gardens, *portales,* and COLORS! At times, they may require some remodeling to enlarge or add rooms, a new coat of paint, and other maintenance issues, but if elevations and interiors are designed traditionally, they should warrant no other updating. In contrast, I remember my 1970's contemporary style home with its chocolate brown shag car-peting, painted kitchen cabinetry (lime green and lemon yellow) and green laminated countertops. I also remember a few years later when all of that was out of style. Traditional Mexican homes are design classics and their timeless beauty never goes out of vogue.

A final note: Even though many hurdles were cleared to complete this project, I will never be a track star. One hour after photographing the final home in San Miguel (the final hurdle), I stumbled and fell, which resulted in a broken foot and an added bonus of torn ligaments. Being bed-ridden for several weeks did have its benefits though—I directed my full attention to writing, and therefore both books were ahead of schedule by several months. This was not an easy race to run, but I believe that *Traditional Mexican Style: Interiors* and *Traditional Mexican Style: Exteriors* are worthy of the effort spent.

Photographer's Preface

Growing up in Wilmington, Delaware, blessed with parents who continually stood by me, allowed me to reach for my dreams. Fond memories of my childhood include my father's basement where he built me a photographic darkroom so that I could explore my newfound hobby. It was also in this dusty environment where my second passion developed. I remember searching through my dad's scrap bin to find two pieces of wood that when together would form some utilitarian function. Both of these hobbies illustrated my desire for creative expression and two interesting careers were born from that Delaware basement.

In 1995, Donna McMenamin approached me with an unusual project. She was working on a book and needed approximately three hundred Mexican art objects photographed, in six different cities and had allotted ten days for the shoot. Needless to say, the thought of actually accomplishing this feat seemed difficult—if not impossible! However, I accepted the challenge and for the next week and a half, I was exposed to a new world that I never knew existed. I fell in love with straw mosaics and the graphics of Tlaquepaque style pottery and knew in an instant that I wanted to collect these two Mexican art forms.

It was not until my work began on *Traditional Mexican Style: Interiors* and *Traditional Mexican Style: Exteriors* that I truly gained an appreciation for the art objects that I had photographed in *Popular Arts*. With San Miguel being home to many outstanding artists and craftsmen, opportunities arose that afforded us close-up observations of works in progress. Just watching the *maestros* carving *cantera* stone and wood, hammering copper, painting pottery/tiles, and punching tin was an unexpected and added bonus. My appreciation for their workmanship grew as I photographed *talavera*-tiled kitchens and bathrooms, carved doors, *cantera,* tinwork, and all of the various art objects installed and displayed in homes throughout these two books.

Being a self-taught furniture maker, I know firsthand what it takes to master a craft and everywhere I looked in these homes, I could see the various artisans' hands at work. In the United States, we are accustomed to construction styles that are somewhat sterile, square, and plumb and we did not witness much of this in Mexico. Not to say everything is off-kilter—on the contrary! Most everything we saw had curving lines, vaulted brick ceilings, elaborate tile work, color, color, and more color! What I love best about the Mexican style is that nothing is exactly perfect, which is a wonderful by-product of something truly handmade.

A traditional Mexican style home is very addicting. Although I own an early American Bungalow that will be fully furnished with my own handmade Arts & Crafts furniture, I cannot help but wonder which room is going to get the full Mexican style treatment!

Enjoy!

Contents

Opposite page:
Talavera place settings (by *Uriarte)* and cobalt hand-blown glasses await an intimate dinner. Chargers by Delores Hidalgo artist Gorky Gonzalez are artfully arranged on the Mexican console. Suspended between the beams (*vigas)* is an elaborate iron chandelier. Fresh-cut flowers add the finishing touch to the elegant setting. *La Casa que Abraza el Cielo.*

Defining the Mexican Style Home

The following transcript is from the author's interview, on January 30, 2002, with Mexican architect Rafael Rios-Ghinis, in Tucson, Arizona. Mr. Rios-Ghinis was born in Acapulco, Guerrero. He graduated in 1975 with a Bachelors' Degree in Architecture from UNAM (University National Autonomous of Mexico) and in 1980 earned a Master's Degree in Architecture from the University of Arizona. He is a member of the Mexican Institute of Architects and is a Licensed Commercial and Residential General Contractor in the State of Arizona. Rafael Rios-Ghinis designed *Casa del Sol y Luna*, one of the homes featured in this and the companion book.

McMenamin—How would you define the Mexican style home?

Ghinis—My perception of the Mexican style home is a vivid universe of visual form: spaces, textures, colors, and decorative elements fusing together into what I call *Archisculpture*. When you put together all of the architectural decorative elements, along with *nichos*, lighting effects, and the building itself, that is the result.

McMenamin—Specifically, what are some of those decorative elements?

Ghinis—For the most part, Mexican houses employ architectural elements such as: column-supported arcades, *nichos*, enclosed courtyards, open spaces, *cúpulas* or domes, patios and fountains, gardens, mosaic walls, wood carved doors, *teja* or Mission tile roofs, Saltillo, cobblestone or brick floors, *portales*, ornate fireplaces and chimneys, stairways and ornamental wrought iron.

McMenamin—That is quite a few details. Would you say that a Mexican style home is more expensive to design and build compared to other architectural styles such as a Contemporary or Santa Fe style home?

Ghinis—Yes on both counts. The traditional Mexican style home uses a great range of diversity and detailed architectural elements, much more than those used in Contemporary and Santa Fe style homes. This requires more time for the architect in the design process, and a greater variety of artisans to carry though the designs, which nowadays is more expensive and difficult to find. All of this makes the task of building and designing the Mexican home more costly. For example, in Santa Fe or Pueblo style architecture, the style is very simple and straightforward. The basic details are round wooden *vigas*, exposed beams in ceilings, lintels, rounded corners, and plastering. With Contemporary style architecture, it is even simpler than that—very straightforward basic lines. Nei-

ther of these styles has as a dramatic visual scale impact as Mexican architecture. All of the decorative elements in the Mexican house drive the cost up with details such as wrought iron, carved wood, *talavera* tile, murals and frescoes, *cantera* stone, and *conchas*. However, it is these details that make the house more interesting, from the architectural point of view, and add to the heightened effects, but carry a higher price tag.

McMenamin—As you know, we photographed houses in San Miguel and Tucson for this project. While Mexican houses on both sides of the border are similar, there are marked architectural differences between the two. Would you agree that the American version of the Mexican house is very different from our counterparts in Mexico?

Ghinis—In many respects, they are different. The American version of the Mexican house has been modified by conditions such as climate, construction materials, and modern lifestyles with special consideration on comfort and convenience. For example, in Mexico, the house design relies heavily on orientation and natural cross ventilation for climate control, while the American counterpart uses mechanical equipment. Another major difference is in the use of color. In Mexico, houses are frequently rich in color, which places an important design factor in its architecture while the American version diminishes this expressive and vivid quality of the house. However, I believe this apprehension to color is abating and slowly is being adapted and welcomed as a sincere and honest design element that governs in the Mexican Spanish tradition.

McMenamin—I agree with that last statement as well. I see from all the latest decorating magazines that Americans are beginning to use lots of color in their interior space, no matter the architectural style. Faux painting seems to be all the rage and while today's designers may consider this a trend, I hope it continues. I think that Americans are enjoying their colored walls as Mexicans have done for centuries.

Ghinis—Not only that, it is an intricate and a very important design element that goes along with the architecture. So, Donna, when are you going to paint your interior walls (ha, ha)?

McMenamin—That is my next project. Americans may be painting their interior walls in beautiful colors, but I do not see that happening on the exterior walls, with the exception of the barrios. Why do you think that is?

Ghinis—I think the government officials and homeowner associations unfortunately dictate that situation, while in Mexico, on the other hand, you have total freedom and the flexibility to use any color scheme.

McMenamin—One thing Americans love about Mexico, is that the Mexican people are not afraid to use color and they seem to have an excellent color sense. They are masters at juxtaposing one color against another.

Ghinis—That is true. It is too bad we do not have the freedom to do that here, but I believe that little by little that homeowners and even government officials are becoming acquainted and more open minded to this aspect of Mexican architecture. One vivid example that utilizes striking colors is the *Placita*, in downtown Tucson. It is very nice and welcome to see someone taking into consideration that important aspect of design.

McMenamin—We seem to have a greater concentration of Mexican homes in the Sunbelt states of Texas, Arizona, Florida, and California. Is there a reason for that?

Ghinis—Without getting into the historical part of it, I think this type of house is more suitable for warm and sunny climates, due to the nature of the architectural style, which is for the most part, to enjoy outdoor living. There is also the aspect of Spanish cultural backgrounds bringing prevailing values and traditions.

McMenamin—Do you feel that Arizona, Texas, and California's close proximity to Mexico has any consideration?

Ghinis—Yes, but I would also include Florida in this because of its tropical climate, which is very appropriate for this style. Mexican houses seem to be born from the physical conditions of the surroundings. The surroundings have a positive impact on the design of the house itself. They play off each other. Oftentimes, you do not have to do very much additional landscaping as the terrain is already in place from semi-tropical to desert surroundings and that requires very little work to incorporate courtyards, fountains and wall mosaics.

McMenamin—What are the architectural design elements and characteristics in the Spanish Colonial home?

Ghinis—A Spanish Colonial house is U or L shaped and designed around a patio or courtyard and is usually secluded from the outer world with fortress-like exterior walls. It is specifically designed to create a private atmosphere to enjoy living outdoors, complete with all of its socializing and entertaining. *Portales* and *corredores*, built up with arcades and columns, surround the central court and all of the social activity rotates around this area. Additionally most rooms of the house open to the *portal*, not only to provide instant access to the outside, but also to serve as passageways to other rooms of the house.

McMenamin—While many Mexican style homes in the States have several of the elements that you describe, there seems to be a marked difference in the exterior elevations. Can you comment on this?

Ghinis—In Mexico, the Spanish settled mainly in what are the downtown areas of the city. Because of the lack of available land space, there is one house after another, separated by a common wall. It lends itself to a fortress-like effect. Therefore, from the street *fachada*, it all looks like one continual tall wall separated only by different colors. It is the interior elevations that receive all of the architectural details, those can only be seen once you enter the home from the street. In Mexico, you are concentrated in your indoor courtyard area so all of the interesting elevations are focused on that particular focal point. On the other hand, in the States, while we have certain codes and regulations we must adhere to, we also have the added bonus of land. The land affords us space between homes, and allows architects to design four exterior elevations. However, the architect must be cognizant of the building site and surrounding terrain and all that it offers. In Tucson, for example, most new construction sites come with acreage and may offer incredible city and/or mountain views. If I designed a typical Spanish Colonial U-shaped home with all rooms opening up to the central courtyard, the home's walls would totally shroud the views, which would be a disaster and disservice to the clients. Architects must consider all that a particular building site and its topography has to offer, and plan his design according to all of these factors. Materials also play an important role in designing the elevations. In Mexico, we have a larger variety of natural materials to work with like volcanic rock and *cantera* stone. These elements, in many colors, can enrich the facade and that can make a huge difference.

McMenamin—Can you tell us something about *cantera* stone?

Ghinis—*Cantera* is a very soft volcanic stone that we find in various states in Mexico including Saltillo, Queretaro, Jalisco, and Michoacán. Depending on the region, it comes in a variety of colors—peaches, grays, browns, pinks and black. It holds up well with exterior use and the weather actually seems to enrich it. An abundance of *maestros* expertly carves this stone and there seems to be no limit to their imagination, or any motif too difficult to attempt. *Cantera* adorns homes all over Mexico surrounding doorways, fireplaces, and windows. There is also a host of freestanding sculptures, fountains, columns, and flooring made from *cantera*.

McMenamin—Can you provide one or two key design/decorating elements for each of the following?

Ghinis—*Sala*—It should be designed adjacent to the *portal*, to facilitate easy interaction in both areas and furnished with massive furniture and a fireplace, often including *cantera* and *talavera* surrounds.

Cocina—The kitchen surroundings should be appealing to the eye as it is usually the hub of activity. A *brasero* and its hood are important focal points along with niches, *alacenas*, and enumerable *talavera* wall and counter surface treatments.

Comedor—I want to see a beautiful chandelier over the table.

Recámaras—Three good focal points in the bedroom could be the headboard, a niche or plaster shell, and a fireplace. Most bedrooms in Mexico have an elaborate fireplace and the headboards are of carved wood, tin, or wrought iron. Appropriate lamps would include those of iron, clay, brass, or tin.

Techos y pisos—Concerning the *bóveda* ceiling, it is widely used in the state of Jalisco and the masons use brick, overlapping it over steel beams (which is hardly noticeable after the work is done) which creates its outstanding look. We do not see it as much now, as the price is cost prohibitive and many of the creative masons have moved to other lines of work, due to its lack of demand. Other good decorative ceiling treatments include installing *talavera* between beams and painted murals. For flooring, Saltillo is widely used and others include brick, cobblestone, colored concrete, and slate.

Escaleras—*Talavera* risers with wrought iron balustrades. Tile brings with it an infinite variety of color and design possibilities.

Puertas—Becomes a prelude for the architectural elements that the house is going to exhibit. May be carved or of wrought iron.

Baños—I like to try to use design elements that resemble water by using blue or turquoise colors and by the addition of mermaids, fish, and *conchas*. The bathroom is a perfect room to use a *talavera* mosaic effect. If there is an opportunity for an inside garden, I like to put one in the bathroom. Traditional surface treatments would include *talavera*, although we are beginning to see the use of slate, travertine, marble and polished concrete.

Iluminación—Mexican artisans create infinite varieties of light fixtures in brass, copper, tin, wrought iron, and ceramic. Used properly, they combine with other architectural details to produce striking effects.

Artes—The Mexican house is very bold in the architectural sense and when the accessories work with the home's details, the result is magnificent.

Columnas—Columns styles are square, round, elaborate, or with sincere simplicity and are constructed of wood, *cantera*, concrete, or brick.

Nichos—Affords the perfect opportunity to utilize dead spaces. Tiled or painted backgrounds enhance the *Santos* and *Cristos* within.

Albercas—Pools enhance the architecture and become a perfect location for displaying *cantera* pots and sculptures.

McMenamin.—I know the readers will find your responses both informative and enlightening. *Muchas gracias* for helping us with this project.

The master bedroom's corner fireplace is a wonderful example of creating two visually contrasting patterns with the same tile—the *medio-pañuelo* patterned tile. The surround has been set in a diamond design and the hearth's facing was laid in a herringbone pattern. One tile—two different looks! *Casa de la Condessa.*

Chapter 1.
Entryways- *Entradas*

Entryways to the Mexican houses in San Miguel, Guanajuato, Mexico, and Tucson, Arizona, differ greatly. In San Miguel, most of the homes have an enclosed passageway, referred to as a *zaguán,* which leads visitors from the street into the home's interior courtyard. *Zaguánes* are often quite dramatic, as you will see from the photographs.

Entryways of Tucson Mexican style homes are usually open vestibules, which afford guests a first glimpse of the home's interior.

In each home, north or south of the international border, the diversity and the beauty of the *zaguán*/vestibule is never overlooked. It is, after all, largely responsible for the all-important first impressions of the *casa*.

Love thy neighbor, in this instance, means love his wall! The interior stone wall, by the side of the stairway (*escalera*), is the three-hundred-year-old exterior wall of the neighboring convent. The normal practice is to plaster over these walls, but in this case it was left natural, adding a strong appearance to the stairway. An old priest's vestment, displayed on the wall, is a fitting decorative addition. *Estrella de la Mañana.*

A six-foot-tall San Francisco de Assisi figure, of sabino wood, captivates visitors entering the vestibule (*vestibulo*) from the carved double doors. Saltillo flooring is installed at the doorway, but the floor changes to oak as you enter the Great room. *Casa de Wachs*.

Opposite page:
The entry hall, which serves as the main artery of this home, received a total facelift. Plaster architectural elements were added around the arched openings and above and below the new niche. Finishing touches were accomplished by two of Tucson's local artists. Walls were faux painted by Todd Karleskein, and Frank Franklin further embellished the niche with a fresco. *La Casa Lomita Linda*.

A tall pair of candlesticks stand alongside an old carved bench in the passageway from the street to the inner courtyard (*zaguán*). A vintage oil-on-canvas painting hangs above. *Estrella de la Mañana.*

Contrasting paint tones create a heightened visual excitement from this angle of the Great room into the vestibule. The Guatemalan rug, with its bird motif, was discovered at the Pasadena City College antique market and protects the oak entry flooring. A large bas-relief panel, in an alcove, is flanked by tall iron candlesticks. The votive candleholder, made of brass and copper, was found in a New York antique shop. Paint, see Appendix 2: Dunn-Edwards® Crimson and Fenbrook. *Red Thunder Ranch.*

The excellent craftsmanship of architectural details is obvious in this home. Diligence is apparent in the selection of the size, coloring, and form of each rock composing the stone wall, and the *cantera* stone stairway is beautifully constructed. *Casa Heyne.*

Although darkness engulfs the visitor after crossing the threshold, advancing a step or two triggers motion-sensor lighting, and an incredible drama begins to unfold. Besides the arched ceiling, iron grated niches are illuminated to reveal an exquisite collection of masks, one in each of the twenty niches. As you reach each succeeding tier (three in all) of the passageway, the previous tier fades to black. (The owners of this bed and breakfast don't get overly concerned when a visitor hasn't reached the top of the stairs within a couple of minutes. After all, it takes quite a while to enjoy the breathtaking show along the way). *Casa de la Cuesta.*

Opposite page:
With each ascent of the thirty-two steps, more architectural details become visible. A quarry stone baseboard (*cantera zoclo)* runs alongside the steps, plant filled niches are hand painted and enhanced by *cantera* crowns (*coronas*), and the *arista bóveda* ceiling has been faux painted with an intricate diamond design. *Casa Heyne.*

This view greets visitors as they come through the front door. A well-placed mirror, planter box, and a huge *cantera* stone San Jorge figure work together to create a strong focal point at the end of the passageway. *Casa de los Perros.*

Immediately upon entering the passageway, with its profusion of colors, one feels the influence of the well-known Mexican architect, Luis Barragán. A contemporary red wall fountain tumbles water into a lower basin. A lone Mexican table, commanding center stage, is decorated with colorful glass balls, while planted *talavera* flower-pots *(macetas)* soften the whole effect. *Casa de Reinhart.*

At the opposing end of the passageway, two prominent contemporary folk art sculptures, (right side) *No Flowers* and (left side) *Ugly Daughter* by American artist Lester Van Winkle, complement the vibrant pink walls. A beautiful wrought iron gate can be locked, allowing the front doors to remain open. *Casa de Reinhart.*

Chapter 2.
Living Rooms- *Salas*

Filled with comfortable furnishings, such as leather and southwest-themed-fabric sofas and chairs, living rooms reflect the homeowners' personal tastes like no other. Whether formal or casual decor is chosen for the furnishings, the living room is an ideal choice to showplace personal collections.

Throughout the home's interior, the use of solid walls was kept to an absolute minimum, due to the incredible three-hundred-sixty-degree vistas and the owners' desire for open, airy spaces. From a second conversation area in the Great room, separation of space was accomplished by the use of Tarascan hand-carved posts, open archways, and stepped-down walls. Prominently displayed on the tiled benches (*bancos*) are large vintage Tonaltecan burnished jars (*jarrones*). *Casa del Sol y Luna*.

A corner faux-painted fireplace anchors the Great room that is overflowing with vintage Mexican folk arts. Burnished jars, from Tonalá, bedeck the owner-designed corner cupboard, which doubles as an entertainment center. A pair of old bas-relief painted shutters, reportedly salvaged from a Santa Fe school, were set into the cupboard's upper double doors. Hand-distressed Douglas fir beams and pine planks firmly support the black iron ceiling fans. *Casa del Sol y Luna*.

Rich color provides a joyous backdrop for the owners' collection of Mexican folk arts. A painted wooden mermaid hangs suspended from the plank and beam ceiling. An abundance of masks, carved in the state of Guerrero, and other Mexican folk arts add to the alluring charm. The fireplace (*chimenea*) is spattered with *talavera* tile and fitted with a custom hand-forged iron screen. The carved pine door is from Michoacán. Paint: Dunn-Edwards® Mayan. *Casa de Ghinis*.

It has been more than twenty-five years since the owner first bought a Mexican religious painting (*retablo*). Now the living room walls are blanketed with an impressive collection. The open doorway provides a glimpse into the breakfast room, where more Mexican folk art is displayed. *Casa de Anonymous*.

Opposite page:
During the room's remodeling, the Douglas fir beams and corbels were sandblasted and artist Kay Steinhilper added fresco treatments around the windows. The fireplace received a total face-lift, and Frank Franklin's artistry now rest on the hearth and mantle. *La Casa Lomita Linda*.

The arched entrance features a plaster relief by Kay Steinhilper. Another prized possession, a signed painting by Mario Cruz, hangs over the console table that is topped with Frank Franklin's sculptures. Other native paintings grace the walls, reflecting the owners' love of traditional Mexican arts. *La Casa Lomita Linda*.

A collection of wood, clay, and iron crosses and old Mexican *Santos* decorate this hallway. The large custom-made mahogany entertainment center showcases an array of *talavera* pieces, while distressed fir beams span the ceiling. All of the home's masonry interior walls were plastered and faux finished. *Casa de Wachs*.

Adjacent and open to the kitchen, the family room offers a cozy place to read a book or watch television. The built-in pine entertainment center hides the "tube" and offers storage for books and collections. *Casa de Moser.*

Below:
Nothing spells drama quite like bold red walls, and this huge room should receive an award for vibrancy. A pair of niches (*nichos*), flanking the fireplace, house books and collectibles. The red sofas, on oak flooring, are piled high with patterned pillows for texture and contrast. The archway leads to the kitchen and dining areas, and don't miss the wonderful iron screen in front of the fireplace. Paint: Dunn-Edwards® Crimson. *Red Thunder Ranch.*

A Mexican wooden Christ figure (*Cristo*) makes a strong image on this wall. Displayed on the sofa table are pre-Columbian figures and an antique wooden angel. *Casa de Black*.

Pedro Friedeberg fabricated the sofa and chairs in this living room (*sala*). The pair of alter vases, once used in a Mexican church, have been turned into a pair of floor lamps to illuminate the wonderful Tlaquepaque-inspired, hand-painted murals by Lisa Mellinger of San Antonio, Texas. The Linares family is responsible for the papier-maché Day of the Dead figure on the coffee table. The flooring is flagstone. *Casa de Roberts*.

Situated in front of the fireplace, at one end of the living room, a pigskin (*equipale*) table and chairs create an intimate space. An arrangement of dried eucalyptus look terrific, arranged in a large *talavera* jar. Two alter pieces on the stone mantle, set off the *talavera* bowl. *Casa Hidalgo*.

An eighteenth-century wooden figural rendition of *La Immaculata*, from Paraguay, presides over this living room from a pedestal. Resting on the fireplace mantle and in the niche (*nicho),* the vintage burnished jars are from Tonalá. The flooring is stained concrete and Saltillo tile is on the stairway. *Casa de Clark*.

Massive *cantera* stone columns flank the opening to the opposing end of this living room. An old leather suitcase serves as a coffee table on the ancient stone floor and built-in benches (*bancos*) provide seating. The firebox facade is *cantera* laid in a herringbone pattern. *Casa Hidalgo*.

Chapter 3.
Kitchens- *Cocinas*

Considered by many homeowners to be the most important room in the home, the Mexican style kitchen is always a hub of activity. It is the premier gathering place for family and friends.

A major difference observed between the San Miguel and Tucson kitchens is the cooking area (*brasero*)—an important design component of a traditional Mexican kitchen. Gas burners are set into the top surface (usually made with *talavera* tile) and the controls protrude through the front facade. Certain building codes in the United States may prevent this type of assembly, but a similar look can be achieved by constructing a *brasero* and adding a surface gas cooktop unit. (The kitchen in *Casa del Sol y Luna* is a good example of using this method.)

Pine cabinetry, *talavera* tile, and Saltillo flooring are used throughout Mexican-style kitchens. And no traditional Mexican kitchen would be complete without a hearty dose of Mexican pottery—a staple no matter where you live!

Adding further architectural interest to the kitchen is the bricked archway that crowns the casement windows. The backsplash tile treatment's half-handkerchief (*medio-pañuelo*) diamond design differs from the counter surface tile, but the same colors are used for uniformity. *Casa de la Condessa.*

Opposite page:
One side of the galley-style kitchen features an open arched, checkerboard tiled counter with the gas stove, oven, and refrigerator at the end. Large decorative *talavera* jars occupy the space underneath, adding a touch of blue to the color scheme. An eye-catching, diamond-patterned backsplash half-handkerchief (*medio-pañuelo*) tile contrasts in pattern from the surface tile to create an interesting optical effect. Ideally situated between the two working sides of the kitchen is a small table. *Casa de la Condessa.*

Opposite page:
Two ovens and a warming oven are built-in beneath the *talavera*-tiled buffet. Hot dishes can be removed from the oven and placed directly onto the tiled surface without fear of harming the tile. A gas cook-top and a cobalt blue vegetable sink leave plenty of preparation space on the center island. Custom-crafted, faux finished Mexican cedar cabinets were made in Mexico by Salvador Orozco. *La Flor del Desierto.*

Light emitting from the stained glass quatrefoil window keeps the kitchen brightly lit. The breakfast bar's combination of *talavera*-tiled countertops over the lattice, cedar-strip base is unusual and charming. It is a perfect complement to the pigskin (*equipale*) bar stools. A small iron shelf showcases papier-maché fruit. *Casa de Ghinis.*

If you think Saltillo tile is only for floors, you may want to re-think that position. Take a closer look at the countertop in the fore-ground. This Saltillo countertop, trimmed in cobalt blue *talavera*, combine handsomely with the alder wood custom cabinetry. The kitchen's blue and white color scheme is composed of half-handkerchief tiles (*medio-pañuelo talavera*) laid in an eclipsing square pattern. Closer inspection of the niche reveals a *talavera* mural set into the wall. *Casa de Robinson.*

Black floral painted trays (*bateas*) from Olinalá, visibly dominate the ocher walls above the richly stained pine custom cabinetry in this open-concept kitchen. Six-inch square *talavera* tiles were used in lieu of the usual four-inch size to cover the countertops and island. The shallow niche at one end of the island is a perfect place to display the wooden animal from Oaxaca. Paint: Dunn-Edwards® T.J. Water and Rio Fleece. *Casa de Wachs.*

Alongside the pantry's pine double door ticks an oak grandfather clock that was transformed into a wonderfully folksy piece after being faux painted by a friend of the owners. (Its charming quality captivated us; we predict a run on oak clocks.) *Casa de Wachs.*

The owner's decorator utilized several surface treatments in the finishing touches to this open-concept kitchen. The double-sink's island top is made from granite, and concrete was used on all the others. *Talavera* tile, by Uriarte, covers the backsplash walls and intensifies the coffer. Cherry custom cabinetry adds warmth and offers display areas for some of the owner's art collection. *La Casa que Abraza el Cielo.*

A stainless steel gas stove was covered by a stucco hood that was beautifully scripted to read, "*Danos el pan nuestro de cada día*" *(*Give us our daily bread*)*. Tile-covered walls were carefully designed to insure that the six-inch tiles would require absolutely no cutting. *La Casa que Abraza el Cielo.*

In this open-concept kitchen, the stucco and *talavera* tiled *brasero* is typical of colonial Mexico, but is equipped with the modern-day convenience of a natural gas cooking top. Cookware is kept handy in the tiled niches underneath. A panel of *talavera,* set into the hood, is the work of the Guevara family of Puebla. *Casa del Sol y Luna.*

The architect designed the island's unusual configuration after an old Aztec design. The butcherblock top was custom crafted, as was the cabinetry, by 4 Brothers Cabinetry. There are two sets of four graduated drawers, three blind cabinets, and open shelving for cookbooks at the opposite end. All of the iron hardware was commissioned in Mexico. Six pictorial painted doors open to the butler's pantry, and an old *Corona* beer cooler, repainted with a folksy Mexican scene, rests underneath. The gallery hallway leads to the home office. *Casa del Sol y Luna.*

Our homeowner, Roger, works in the *before* kitchen that was destined for oblivion. The vent-a-hood and dark oak cabinets were changed. In the *after* photo, a point of reference is the kitchen window to Roger's left. *La Casa Lomita Linda. Photograph courtesy of the owners.*

What a fabulous transformation—it really is the same kitchen! The mesquite-topped island houses two single ovens and a trash compactor. Gleaming copper cookery hangs from iron hooks on the fir beams. Custom pine lower cabinets, headed by *talavera* tile, replaced the old stock cabinets. *La Casa Lomita Linda.*

Beautifully painted upper and lower cabinetry in this U-shaped kitchen were coordinated to match the predominately green and white *talavera* tile. A splash of cobalt blue is introduced with a small portion of the counter surface tile and the herringbone design of the half-handkerchief (*medio-pañuelo*) tile design behind the stove. Note the spice niche on the left wall. *Casa de los Perros*.

In a traditional U-shaped kitchen, an old wooden beam functions as a lintel over the *brasero*. Colored and polished cement counter surfaces are highlighted by a *talavera* tile border. The carved, overhead cupboard stores a sundry of kitchen necessities. *Casa Hidalgo*.

A kitchen is an ideal place for displaying one's addiction for vintage Mexican pottery. Pine cabinetry, some with stained glass fronts (found at *La Ganilla*—the thieve's market), are charmingly decked with pottery from the states of Jalisco and Michoacán—a great display of regional flavor! *Casa de Roberts*.

Douglas fir beams and honey-colored pine custom cabinetry offer warmth and balance the Saltillo flooring and *talavera* tile counter tops in this open-concept kitchen. Mexican folk arts are featured above the cabinetry and on the walls. *Casa de Moser*.

A charming U-shaped kitchen where the kitchen's tile work is a conglomerate of unmatched blue and white *talavera* tiles. The owner professed that it was a labor of love to diligently seek out every example of a blue and white tile that could be found. It is a fabulous look! *Talavera* jars sit on top of the carved pine cabinets. *Estrella de la Mañana.*

With six burners on this *brasero*, a lot of dishes can be accomplished easily. Note that the position of the controls on front is the traditional placement. *Estrella de la Mañana.*

Detail of a wall cupboard (*alacena*) bordering the kitchen door, used to prominently display *talavera* place settings. *Estrella de la Mañana.*

In Spanish Colonial times, there were no overhead cabinets. Instead, the Spanish used the built-in wall cupboards (*alacenas*) (left) or hanging open shelves (*repisas*) and other small cupboards. An American Arts & Crafts vase sits on the old pine table. *Estrella de la Mañana.*

This *brasero* includes everything on a cook's wish list. Moving from left to right, there is a deep fat fryer, a griddle, a grill, and gas burners. The pine, spindel turned cabinetry to the left of the *brasero* ends with an under-counter oven. A herringbone-patterned mesquite table serves as the center island. An incredible domed ceiling vaults over the kitchen. The floor and ceiling are covered with *talavera* tiles. (We counted over eight different tile patterns used in this kitchen.) *Casa Heyne*.

Opposite the cooking area, lots of storage space exists in pine lower cabinetry and cupboards. Two wooden casement windows and iron chandeliers supply the lighting. A beautiful finishing detail is the ceiling's five-tier step-down. *Casa Heyne.*

In this kitchen, it is logical that the jambs and sills of the recessed casement windows receive the same decorative treatment. Additionally, there is another side to this O-shaped kitchen, which contains three more sinks. *Casa Heyne.*

Eight gas burners on the *brasero* are more than most chefs will ever need, but they provide enviable space for creativity. The polished cement countertop looks terrific with cobalt blue and white tile. The hood is adorned with *medio-pañuelo* tile laid in a diamond pattern. Folk art toys and *talavera* jars sit on the running shelving. *Casa de la Cuesta.*

A kitchen in the owners' private small house (*casita*) sits adjacent to their living room. *Medio-pañuelo talavera* tiles, in the eclipsing squares pattern, line the outside edge of the polished cement countertop and switch to a diamond pattern inside the niche. The hood was painted to coordinate with the tile color. A deep blue painted cement ledge is wide enough for an ever-changing display of Mexican folk art. In this instance, unsigned clay *catrinas* hold court. The new floors were prepared with kerosene and tar pitch for coloring and finished with many coats of floor wax. *Casa de la Cuesta.*

Chapter 4.
Dining Rooms- *Comedores*

Dining room ambiance in the traditional Mexican style house runs the gamut between formal and casual. Fireplaces are commonplace, as are beautiful chandeliers and furnishings. Pigskin (*equipale*) and hand-carved wooden chairs encircle tables fabricated from pine, mesquite, or sabino wood. Candelabras cast romantic shadows across *talavera* dishes and hand-blown glass, silver, and pewter goblets. The Mexican-style dining room is that special place for family and friends to enjoy good food and lively conversation.

An old cut-down, tin-topped cheese table performs as a dining room table with seating for ten. Hanging above the fireplace is a captivating oil on canvas painting by Canadian artist, Marion Perlet, who now resides in San Miguel, Mexico. Opposite are windows and French doors that open to the porch (*portal);* in San Miguel's ideal climate, these are open almost year round. *Casa Chorro.*

At one end of the dining room, an old plate rack hangs above an intricately carved buffet, providing a perfect place to display vintage *talavera*, Tlaquepaque pottery, and lacquerware from Olinalá. Closer inspection of the table reveals old blue paint and a good look at the tin top. *Casa Chorro.*

The opposing end of the dining room showcases a companion painting by Perlet and an incredible, six-foot-high, oil on canvas painting of the Virgin of the Guadalupe, patron saint of the Americas. Fresh flowers and flaming candelabras set a delightful mood for dinner guests. *Casa Chorro.*

The carved secretary fits perfectly into a recess in the breakfast room (*desayunador*). The vertical row of niches is put to good use housing the television and art objects. Paint: Dunn-Edwards® T.J. Water and Rio Fleece. *Casa de Wachs*.

The kitchen flows into the brightly colored and absolutely charming dining room. While the table seats six comfortably, a built-in bench stands ready to handle any overflow. A myriad of star-shaped, punched tin and glass lights dangle over the table, which is set with *talavera* place settings and hand-blown glasses. *Casa de la Condessa*.

Avid collectors of Mexican antiques, the owners' dining room displays a museum-caliber collection of nineteenth-century religious paintings (*retablos*) and burnished pottery from Tonalá. Suspended from the fifteen-foot ceiling, an iron chandelier illuminates the seventeenth-century, Italian trestle table and vintage pottery jar from Tlaquepaque. *Casa de Clark*.

Vintage Mexican folk arts anchor one end of the dining room, including trees of life (*arboles de la vida*), made by the Flores family of Izúcar de Matamoras. Also, painted trays (*bateas*) from Olinalá, *talavera* from Puebla, and glazed pottery from Tlaquepaque add warmth to the display. *Casa de Clark*.

The breakfast room's early Mexican store cabinet holds a portion of the owner's fantastic collection of 1920-'30s Tlaquepaque pottery. Vintage painted chairs encircle the table that is set with old Oaxacan pottery. Bas-relief wood panels peek from the right of the store cabinet. *Casa de Clark*.

An unusual and eye-catching architectural detail is found in the octagonal-shaped ceiling and coffer. A six-and-one-half-inch opening was framed-out to accommodate two rows of clay roof tiles (*teja*). This opening was not original to the plans, but was envisioned by the architect during the framing process—it pays to have your architect onsite during construction! Three large pine casement windows, above the built-in bench, offer dinner guests incredible city and mountain views. The dining table and carved chairs were made in Nogales, in the 1960s, and were found in a local Tucson junk shop. The centerpiece is an old wooden bowl filled with vintage Mexican clay fruit banks. An intricately woven, nineteenth-century Saltillo sarape highlights one wall, while recessed lighting and a 1930s iron and *talavera* (Uriarte) chandelier illuminate the room. *Casa del Sol y Luna*.

Guests delight in the fanciful, vintage Mexican folk art pottery amassed by the owner. A bull ring, by the famed artist Candelario Medrano, makes a fine table centerpiece, and burnished chargers by Moisés Rodriguez Bautista adorn the walls. The clay nativity scene is probably the work of Teodora Blanco. *Casa de Anonymous*.

Twelve studded leather chairs surround the massive dining table. The tin cabinet displays the owners' collection of vintage *Mexicana* and *Hacienda* patterned dinnerware by Homer Laughlin. A beautifully carved and painted Mexican mirror hangs above the large buffet and a Mexican tin chandelier provides the lighting. *Casa de Wachs*.

Opposite page:
Talavera place settings (by Uriarte*)* and cobalt hand-blown glasses await an intimate dinner. Chargers by Delores Hidalgo artist Gorky Gonzalez are artfully arranged on the Mexican console. Suspended between the beams (*vigas*) is an elaborate iron chandelier. Fresh-cut flowers add the finishing touch to the elegant setting. *La Casa que Abraza el Cielo.*

Adjacent and open to the kitchen, the breakfast room is outfitted with a raised fireplace, making chilly mornings and evenings a thing of the past. A painted Mexican cupboard houses collections of Fiesta ware. The table is set with random colored Fiesta dishes coupled with colorful placemats. *La Flor del Desierto.*

Above:
By looking from the living area through the archway into the dining room, one notices the green, Mexican, pictorial-painted cabinet against vivid red walls. A large potted euphorbia anchors the corner of the room that is adjacent to the kitchen. *El Castillo*.

Opposite page:
Sitting on the contemporary Mexican table is a Tlaquepaque charger from the 1930s. The two-hundred-year-old Peruvian buffet displays vintage bowls and birds from Tonalá and Tlaquepaque. A Spanish Colonial leather trunk is flanked by Mexican pewter and glass candleholders. *Casa de Black*.

Beneath a Mexican chandelier, ladder-back chairs surround a marble dining table. *The Little Mariachi* painting, by Frank Franklin, graces an end wall. Local faux artist Kay Steinhilper applied the plaster ceiling treatment, and tile borders provide a great finishing touch. The wooden horse's head rests on a *cantera* stone pedestal. *La Casa Lomita Linda*.

A variety of pillow textures and patterns add playfulness to the built-in bench, located adjacent to the kitchen. Both ends of the bench were elevated and covered with *talavera* tile to function as tables. Here, the owner puts them to good use as pedestals for his ever-growing art collection. *Casa Kino*.

A stunning, painted jig-sawed transom caps the turned spindle doors leading from the dining room to the patio. A pigskin-covered *(equipale)* captain's chair heads the richly patinaed table. *Casa Hidalgo.*

This view of one of the two dining areas that flank the kitchen displays the bold area rug, over oak flooring, that unites the vibrant turquoise tiled countertops and painted walls. A built-in bench continues to the corner plastered fireplace, where it is enjoyed by diners and cooks alike. Paint: Dunn-Edwards® Fenbrook (wall) and Swiss Coffee (fireplace). *Red Thunder Ranch.*

Chapter 5.
Bedrooms- *Recámaras*

Bedrooms in Mexican-style *casas* offer more than just a place to sleep at the end of the day. Master bedrooms are the homeowners' private, personal refuge, and as such receive a great deal of individual attention. Many have separate sitting areas, complete with a fireplace and daybed or comfy chairs. An afternoon siesta or hours spent reading is commonplace in these rooms.

Elaborate headboards and footboards in iron, tin or carved wood insure that the bed takes center stage in the bedroom. Beds are dressed with hand-woven bedspreads in cotton or wool, denim comforters and sarapes, or intricate embroidery work. Bedside tables are often a reclaimed chest, an old Monterey, California, table, or are fashioned of *talavera* tile. Varieties of bedside table lamps provide light for reading.

Opposite page:
An innovative use for Tarascan carved columns is this four-poster bed. The *cantera* fireplace lends ambiance and warmth to this master bedroom. *Casa Hidalgo*.

A rainbow of colors help to create this charming master bedroom where art from two generations of the Franklin family hold places of honor. The bas-relief painted double bed bears the signature of Francisco, circa 1985. A pair of oil on canvas paintings, signed by Franklin's daughter Maja, hang prominently on the wall. The floor is brick. Paint: Dunn-Edwards® Bristol (wall) and Pure Butter (trim). *Casa de Franklin*.

Detail of the bed. *Casa de Franklin*.

Right:
Twin beds are dressed in denim comforters in the *Moroca* bedroom. Polly Stark Ortega (from San Miguel) faux painted the walls with a herringbone design. The rock wall is made with excavated material. Be sure and look upwards for a glimpse of the adobe ceiling. *Casa Heyne*.

A pair of clay lamps flanks the iron bed, one on an old chest recycled into a nightstand. A locally acquired cotton bedspread and embroidered pillows dress the bed. *Casa de la Condessa*.

Hand-hammered copper lamps flank a draped, four-poster iron bed in the master bedroom (*recámara principal).* Indirect cove lighting in the vaulted ceiling adds romantic atmosphere. *Casa Heyne.*

The bedroom's blue and white color scheme puts guests at ease. Vintage rugs from Texcoco are scattered over Saltillo tile floors. A 1930s American quilt, signed by its makers, dresses the bed. The *talavera* fireplace surround, using *medio-pañuelo* tile in the herringbone design, contrasts nicely with the striped fabric on the overstuffed chair. *Red Thunder Ranch*.

Embroidered muslin textiles from Morocco are striking against the stark white cotton bedspread and blue walls in the Moroccan bedroom. *Casa Chorro*.

What guest would want to leave accommodations including a microwave oven, refrigerator, and sink built into recessed cabinetry? The owners' son, Mark, hand painted the frieze above the cabinet, matching the backsplash tile pattern perfectly. Paint: Benjamin Moore & Co.® #1364. *Casa de Robinson*.

Below:
Faux painted walls in the master bedroom accentuate the old, hand-painted wedding trunk from Chiapas. A wooden sculpture of *La Santisima Virgin Maria* stands stately in one corner. Over the bed, the Mexican painting is signed by Almendore. *Casa Kino*.

This hand-formed and recessed plastered shell creates a stunning headboard in the master bedroom. Plastered walls beautifully accept the custom-mixed, faux finishing down to the oak floors. The open door leads to the gentlemen's bathroom. *Casa de Wachs*.

Skillfully executed, Sergio Bustamante-style, *papier-maché* masks, from Guadalajara, appear lifelike on ocher, faux-painted bedroom walls. The pine bas-relief headboard is from Michoacán, circa 1960-'70s. Paint: Dunn-Edwards® Butter Up. *Casa de Ghinis*.

In the master bedroom, a beautifully crafted iron, four-poster bed is placed before the *Sueños Cariñosos* (sweet dreams) mural, that depicts a pair of hovering angels. The mural, as well as the fireplace, blanket box, and painting, are the work of Frank Franklin. *La Casa Lomita Linda*.

Open arches, above a distressed lintel, enclose vintage Roadside pottery. Three identically carved Tarascan columns define and separate the sitting area from the sleeping quarters. The dresser, from Chihuahua, showcases more Roadside pottery and Mexican wooden sculptures. *Casa del Sol y Luna*.

The sun pours through the quatrefoil window highlighting the sun and moon design in the guest bedroom. Twin vintage Monterey beds are covered in sarape-patterned comforters. The 1940-'50s painting is by José Maria de Servin. *Casa del Sol y Luna*.

Painted trays (*bateas*) are eye-catching on the walls in this guest bedroom. Building upon the Mexican theme are sarape-covered pillows and chairs. The embroidered pillows were found in San Miguel de Allende. *Casa de Anonymous*.

The green walls serenely set a mood for meditation here. While the space was original to the home, it has been remodeled with new flooring, arched windows, and beamed ceiling. An old Mexican painted trunk, found locally, makes a fine coffee table in front of the antique Guatemalan daybed. *Red Thunder Ranch*.

Local Hispanic artists carved and painted the headboard. The gas fireplace, ingeniously placed between the home office and master bedroom, delivers warmth to both spaces. *Casa de Moser.*

Talavera tiles frame and emphasize the hand-carved, pine doors in the master bedroom. The middle section houses the television. A stairway leads up to more bedrooms on the third level of the home. *Casa de la Condessa.*

A 1930s, Argentinean, iron balcony railing became an interesting headboard for this bed. The 1930-'40s Mexican painting is from the Diego Rivera School of Muralists. A Monterey side table stands next to the bed. *Red Thunder Ranch*.

Painted coconut masks from Guerrero and colorful bedside tables add whimsical charm to this bedroom. *Casa Chorro*.

The marvelously stenciled walls and beautiful tin headboard create an elegant bedroom. *Casa de la Condessa*.

An extraordinary amount of work created this repoussé tin headboard. *Casa de la Condessa*.

An array of brightly painted, differently sized, wooden birdcages brings attention to the adobe brick walls.
Sarapes and embroidered pillows accent the white cotton muslin bedspreads. *Casa Heyne.*

73

Opposite page:
During excavation, a large amount of stone was found that subsequently was recycled back into the house; for example, the corner wall in this bedroom. A *talavera* lamp illuminates a pine table. *Talavera* tile surrounds a section of the window jamb and sill on the left. *Casa Heyne.*

Three carved columns and a lower level divide the master bedroom from the adjoining sitting area. Six carved panels, salvaged from an old Mexican hotel in Yuma, Arizona, have been recycled into the temporary headboard. Cheech, one of the two Siamese cats that own the home, poses on a 1910-'20s Tlaxcala sarape. *Casa del Sol y Luna.*

Red and yellow color schemes are used a great deal in homes throughout Mexico. This bedroom's yellow walls are highlighted by a painted cornice of red stars. The bedside table has red scorpions painted along the border. A vintage Mexican sarape covers the bed. Paint: Dunn-Edwards® Vice Versa and Wineberry. *Red Thunder Ranch*.

In the *Máscaras* bedroom, a striking bedspread was constructed from an existing colorfully hand-embroidered cloth from Puebla and three additional sections of cotton muslin. The center medallion and border are quite unusual. Bark paintings by Ignacia Ramirez hang above the bed. *Casa de la Cuesta*.

Chapter 6.
Bathrooms- *Baños*

"It's just a bathroom" is a phrase that does not fit in this style of home. Bathrooms are recipients of ample architectural and decorative detailing. An extensive use of *talavera* tile, adorns tops of vanities, walls, showers, and bathtubs. The only noticeable difference in Mexican-style bathrooms of Mexico and the United States is the bathtub itself. Masons fabricate the tubs in Mexico from start to finish, while those in the United States usually are the ready-made variety. However, with a little imagination, store-bought tubs can be disguised. The Arizona home, *Casa de Wachs*, illustrates a fine example of disguising the bathtub.

A modern wall-to-wall mirror over the sink, if used at all, can be surrounded with a *talavera*-tiled border. The more traditional decor is hanging mirrors with frames made from iron, tin, or wood.

Alternating mustard and white *talavera* tiles fashion a wonderful, bright checkerboard floor in the bathroom. The tile on the vanity, tub, and wall has been laid in diagonal and rectangular grid patterns. *Talavera* tiles in a variety of mustard tones produce the subtle shading. *Casa de la Cuesta.*

The floor rug inspired a striking color combination for the master bathroom (*baño principal*). Centered over the bathtub is a tiled panel (*tablero*) of the Virgin of the Guadalupe by Gorky Gonzalez, and the *talavera* plates set into the tile wall are also his work. A small gas fireplace, on the right, generates a lot of welcome heat. *Casa Heyne.*

A closer look at the plates by Gorky Gonzalez that are set into the bathroom wall. *Casa Heyne.*

Five shades of *talavera* tiles were set randomly between top and bottom bordering tiles. The much adored herringbone border pattern was created by two rows of *medio-pañuelo talavera*. A functional cabinet, built between the tub and shower, holds towels. The tile-delineated, quatrefoil window furnishes natural light, a most important feature in this lady's bathroom. *Casa de Wachs*.

Opposite page:
Bathrooms in Mexican homes provide an opportunity for creative innovation. The bathtub's dynamic outer wall is designed after a Moorish architectural detail referred to as a *herradura* (horseshoe-shaped) arch. *Casa Heyne.*

A walk-in shower in the Adobe Bathroom utilizes a tile pattern from the vanity with various pictorial tiles to create a charming mixture. Soft light filters through the colorful stained glass casement window. *Casa Heyne.*

The friezes painted on the wall of the Adobe Bathroom are the work of San Miguel artist, Polly Stark Ortega. The unifying effect of the backsplash tile, tin mirrors, and *talavera* sinks make this room appealing. *Casa Heyne.*

Fish (*pescados*) endlessly circle the *talavera* sinks and swim across the top border of the custom stained pine vanity. By a stroke of luck, the owners found six *talavera* pulls for the vanity drawers with identical pattern and coloring as the tiles. Above the sinks are twin tin mirrors. *Casa del Sol y Luna.*

A trio of different *talavera* tiles decorate the walls and built-in bench of this bathroom's walk-in shower. If fish were to swim in the shower walls, they would swim through the quatrefoil window, too. *Casa del Sol y Luna.*

In this bathroom, a wainscot of *talavera* tile mimics surface tile in the open-shelved vanity. Ocher walls accentuate the *medio-pañuelo talavera* that has been installed in a diamond pattern. *Casa Heyne.*

Stepped open shelving separates the toilet from the vanity area and eliminates the need for another door. The owners used several different tiles in the same color schemes for pleasant harmony. *Casa Heyne.*

Bathtubs, in San Miguel homes, are made of concrete in home-made forms, plastered into the desired shape, sealed, and gloriously covered with *talavera* tile. A shower curtain on a brass rod encircles the tub. A tiled terraced wall complements the angle of the open shelving opposite. An entirely different tile pattern has been used at the bottom of the bathtub, creating an eye-catching border. *Casa Heyne.*

The vanity's sinks and tiled top match the bathtub in color and pattern, as a peek into the wooden framed mirrors will show. A collection of tin religious paintings (*retablos*) presides over the colorful walls. *Estrella de la Mañana.*

The walls and window sill exhibit the same patterned tile as the vanity. Using patterned tiles opens up a lot of color options for contrasting tiles and accessories. The owners used a solid cobalt blue tile for the tub's interior, which was an excellent choice for breaking up the pattern. *Estrella de la Mañana.*

A wonderful *talavera* tiled mural strategically placed behind the bathtub is visible from the doorway. *Casa de la Condessa*.

This circular walk-in shower slopes gently from the wall to the drain in the Saltillo floor, catching any water overflow and allowing easy clean-up and maintenance. *Casa de la Condessa*.

Floor-to-ceiling windows, along one side of the tiled bathtub, offer an intimate surrounding. The three-hundred-year-old stone wall is part of the convent next door. Dark green *talavera* tile enhances the richly stained cabinetry. *Estrella de la Mañana.*

A pair of *alacenas* flanking the bathroom vanity contain an array of useful bath items and interesting collections. Deeply carved pine cabinetry offers additional storage. *Casa Hidalgo*.

On the opposite wall, a square bathtub is almost large and deep enough to qualify as a pool. The tile has been extended to the surrounding walls, including the window. A beautiful vaulted (*bóveda*) ceiling encloses the room. *Casa Hidalgo*.

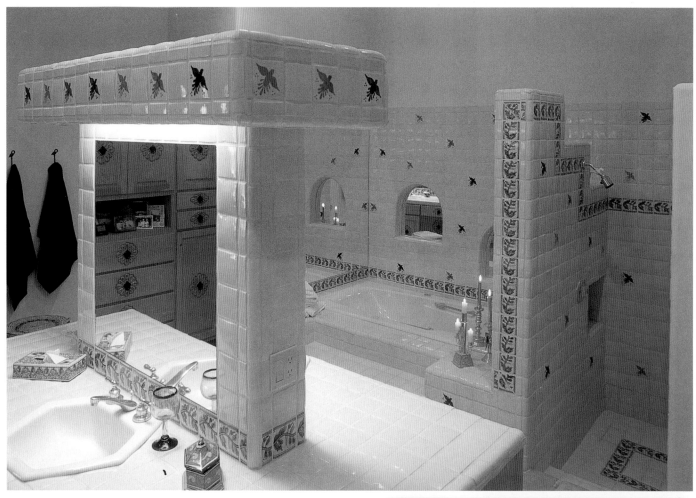

Islands can be just as useful in a bath as they are in a kitchen. In this *talavera*-tiled island in the master bathroom, drawers and doors provide storage for all the bathing necessities. With a dual vanity in the middle, there is space along the perimeter for custom-built-in wardrobe storage. The bathtub and walk-in shower are separated by a tiled terraced wall. *Casa de Moser*.

The pink (*rosa*) and cobalt color combination on the *talavera* sink and tiled backsplash complement the pink *cantera* stone countertops. Once again, we see the delightful result of using the same pattern for sink and tile. *La Casa Lomita Linda*.

Another bathroom features a gently curved wall which eliminates the need for a shower curtain or door. The sink, vanity counter top, and quatrefoil window match the shower's tile design. *Casa del Sol y Luna.*

Detail of the shower's interior floor and walls. *Casa del Sol y Luna*.

Blue and white is a popular color combination in Mexico. Here white is the dominant color with touches of blue in the backsplash tile and sink. *La Flor del Desierto*.

Bathtubs in the United States can be fashioned completely from tile, just like those in Mexico. Here, the bathtub was hand-made and covered with *talavera* tile, along with the wall surrounding it. *La Flor del Desierto*.

Before remodeling, this bath had a dated look and lacked distinctive style. Peer into the mirror's reflection and focus on the wall; then take a look at the classic transformation shown in the next photograph. *La Casa Lomita Linda. Photograph courtesy of the owners.*

Below:
Replacing the existing brown ceramic tile with Saltillo tile updated this powder bath countertop. The backsplash sprang to life with a *medio-pañuelo* tile laid in a sawtooth motif. The same *talavera* tile now frames the mirror and runs along the wainscoting. Featured on the front of the countertop is an innovative bull nose treatment. The owners also replaced the plumbing fixtures and sink, and the mirror reflection reveals the new and attractive wainscoting. A stunning transformation indeed! *La Casa Lomita Linda.*

This small powder bath afforded almost no room for a vanity. A charming solution is the *cantera* stone pedestal that has been inset with a colorful *talavera* sink. Brass fixtures protrude from the *talavera*-tiled wainscoting, preserving premium space on top of the pedestal. *Casa de Robinson*.

The possibilities are endless when coordinating tile colors and patterns. Framing around the mirror is a traditional idea, too! Old style brass hardware provides the finishing touch. *Casa de Robinson*.

Planning and perseverance are key elements in coordinating *talavera* decorative elements in a bathroom. The backsplash, sink, and tile inset into the tin mirror are a good example of this effort. This coordination may take a little more shopping time, but the result is superior. *Casa de Wachs.*

Walls painted deep blue intensify the recessed, hand-formed, white shell above the powder room vanity. A blue and white *talavera* sink coordinates with the white *talavera* surface above richly stained custom cabinetry. *Casa de Wachs.*

A painted antique dresser is out of the ordinary as a sink receptacle, but the result is comfortable and practical. *Casa Hidalgo.*

For this powder bath, a pewter sink and beautiful mirror frame are elegant bright contrasts to the colorful backsplash and surface tile. *La Flor del Desierto.*

The homeowners wanted a window in this powder bathroom, but only interior walls surrounded it. They called on Tucson faux artist, Rebecca Hengsteler, to furnish a desert vista. Adding a pair of shutters completed the trompe l'oeil solution. *Casa de Moser.*

In the House of the Sun and Moon, stars are also featured. In this Bathroom of the Stars (*baño de estrellas*), the counter top, sink, and tin mirror utilize the same star-studded pattern. The sink is the reverse pattern of the counter top. *Casa del Sol y Luna.*

Religious paintings (*retablos*), crosses, and saints (*santos*), interspersed with an old *cantera* stone baptismal font, could make a visit to this powder bath a religious experience. *La Casa que Abraza el Cielo.*

Chapter 7.
Ceilings & Floors- *Techos y Pisos*

Appropriate floor coverings used in Mexican-style homes include Saltillo, brick, *cantera* stone, wood, or concrete. Any of these flooring materials may be used solo or in conjunction with one another. The preference is for Saltillo tile, and this is easily understood since it comes in a variety of shapes and sizes, and can be cut easily by a mason.

Most ceiling treatments incorporate beams in some fashion. Between the beams, a variety of secondary elements may be added, such as brick, planks, *talavera* tile, or paint. Of course, in old Mexico, the *bóveda* (vaulted) ceilings prevail.

Frank A. Smith, a good friend of the owner, hand-painted the ceiling design of intricate geometric diamonds. It spans the width of the ceiling and is, indeed, a work of art among the beams (*vigas*). *Casa Kino*.

A lightweight and absorbent brick, known as *cuña*, makes up this vaulted (*bóveda*) ceiling. The architectural treatment of the three-tiered, step-down cornice is commonly referred to as *pecho de paloma*. Rows of windows supply natural light into this master bathroom. *Casa Heyne.*

While the fir beams and corbels might appear to be adorned with patinaed copper, they are actually the trompe l'oeil painting of local artist, Kay Steinhilper. *La Casa Lomita Linda.*

The glazed tiles (*azulejos*) between the beams were ordinary clay until one of the Mexican jobsite painters began working on them. After painting on the diamond design, a coat of whitewash was applied to give it an antique finish. It beautifully complements the *talavera* tile cornice underneath.*Casa Heyne.*

Opposite page:
Inspired from a traditional design on one of the owner's *talavera* bowls, the porch (*portal*) ceiling was hand-painted by local artists, Bea Wood and Elliott Meadow. *La Casa que Abraza el Cielo.*

Right:
Two local painters began working with the owners on the design for this soaring vaulted ceiling (*arista bóveda*). After trying twenty to thirty samples, they chose this old Moroccan tile pattern. The ceiling rises 65 feet from the floor at the front door and approximately 43 feet from the first floor landing. *Casa Heyne.*

A successful combination of tumbled slate and Saltillo tile created this floor. The double border was designed with an outer row of cut Saltillo and one row of slate. In the center, Saltillo is set on the diagonal, with small tumbled slate as spacers. The painting is by Frank Franklin. *La Casa Lomita Linda*.

Left:
When the original flooring in this section of a hallway needed repair, the owners knew they were not going to be able to match the old tile. A viable and beautiful solution was to lay new *talavera* tile. It looks like it has always been there. *Villa Scorpio al Puente*

Right:
Octagonal Saltillo tile is interspersed with two-inch *talavera* tile with a pebbled border. A four-inch running patterned *talavera* tile is set directly above the Saltillo baseboards. To give this new floor a time-worn look, six to eight coats of linseed oil and thinner were applied to darken it, and then another eight to ten very light applications of floor wax, buffing between each coat. *Casa Heyne*.

The Saltillo tile sun motif was designed and installed by a Mexican master craftsman (*maestro*). Diamond shapes define the border and provide an interesting floor transition. *Casa de Robinson*.

Entrance rugs can often interfere with door openings—this one never will. A faux rug was created with Saltillo tile laid in a diamond pattern, totally contrasting with the direction of the rest of the floor. *Casa de Robinson*.

Chapter 8.
Stairways- *Escaleras*

There is a long-standing tradition of adorning stairways with *talavera* tile. Mexican tile *talleres* produce this tile in infinite patterns and colors, and there are tile factories that will produce custom designs as well. Wrought iron railings often partner with beautiful and colorful tile stairways.

Talavera-tiled risers on this stairway set off the contrasting Ocumicho clay figures of fallen angels (that are transforming into insects). The wall frieze by Lisa Mellinger adds to the stairway's overall enchantment. *Casa de Roberts.*

Cheerful *medio-pañuelo talavera* stair risers, set in a sawtooth design, offer a rainbow of color as the stairway ascends to the roof and garden patio. *Casa de Reinhart*.

Two rows of *medio-pañuelo talavera* tile created this angled stripe pattern in the risers. Normally in the *medio-pañuelo* design, the tile utilizes two solid, contrasting colors, as in the preceding example, but this variation is very appealing as well. *Casa de la Cuesta*.

A variety of *talavera* tiles makes lively risers on this exterior stairway. Rounded *cantera* treads and a twisted iron balustrade provide sure footing and a steady grip for a safe journey to the second floor. *Casa Heyne*.

A bold contrast is achieved between the stained concrete floor and wooden treads by setting the stair risers with tile on a diamond angle. A wooden railing is supported by elaborately twisted, hand-forged, iron uprights (*barandales*). *La Flor del Desierto*.

To separate the cool faux flagstone pool decking from the Saltillo on the porch, the owners installed a row of cobalt blue *talavera* alternating with an eclipse pattern tile on the step riser. *Casa del Sol y Luna.*

Opposite page:
Interchanging a solid tile with a pattern intensifies the design on the stair risers. The balustrade (*balaustrada)* is a beautiful example of Mexican wrought iron work. *Casa del Parque.*

This example and the succeeding one illustrate how a tile pattern can be used differently, depending upon its use. In this example, the floral pattern runs horizontally across the risers. *Casa de Moser.*

At the landing, the same floral tile flanks the stairs vertically, creating a beautiful running border. *Casa de Moser.*

One small detail transforms normal into noteworthy here. The brick steps, with just a touch of cobalt on the risers, make a bold statement at this entrance and coordinate with the *talavera* flowerpot (*maceta*) nearby. *Casa de Wachs*.

This home's alluring charm begins at the front steps. Blue and white *medio-pañuelo talavera* tiles, set in a saw-tooth design on the risers, lead up to the wrought iron gate. The plastered, step-down, low profile walls flanking the steps support matching *talavera* flowerpots. *Casa de Wachs*.

A simple stairway leading to the rooftop is made architecturally interesting by painting the risers deep blue. Below are three "memory" pots, composed of broken ceramics. There is no written information available on memory pots, but the general consensus is that they began being made from a deceased loved one's dishes that were broken and used to decorate a pot or vase *in memorium*. *Casa de la Condessa.*

Three distinct patterns of *talavera* tile on the risers blend beautifully with the colored concrete treads. *La Casa que Abraza el Cielo*.

A spiraling wrought iron stairway leads to the *cantera*-corniced rooftop. The area is laden with containers of trailing African daisies and yellow gazanias. *Casa Heyne*.

Chapter 9.
Niches- *Nichos*

Niches are commonplace in the traditional Mexican home, and an architect may utilize this interesting architectural detail throughout the home, both inside and outside. Homeowners find a multitude of uses for niches, though the traditional one was to house a figure of a favorite Saint.

Saint Francis, a favorite saint in Mexico, is carved from stone and tucked inside this niche (*nicho*) with a good vantage point overlooking the pomegranate tree and fauna. *Casa de Alegret*.

Opposite page:
An elaborate frieze and relief plaster on this niche, which was applied by local artist Kay Steinhilper, is a major focal point of the kitchen entrance. Decoration on this large *talavera* jar inspired her design. *La Casa Lomita Linda*.

This niche is filled with Mexican folk art, including whimsical clay female skeletons that pay tribute to the November 1st and 2nd Day of the Dead celebration. Paint: Benjamin Moore & Co®. #63 and 308. *Casa de Robinson*.

This rectangular tiled mural is original to the home and was produced by The Hispano-Moresque Tile Co. of Los Angeles, California between 1927 and 1932. When the owners remodeled the courtyard years later, one of the workers replicated the tile pattern into the beautifully painted arched border. While this embellishment was not planned, it was welcomed by the owners. *Red Thunder Ranch*.

Opposite page:
A collection of Mexican miniature clay figures are at home in this vibrant niche between the dining room (*comedor*) and kitchen (*cocina*). An application of several layers of paint created the time-worn look on the ocher wall. *Casa de Wachs.*

Right:
In another outdoor niche, a rendition of Saint Michael, carved in *cantera* stone, is highlighted by small, purple, mosaic tile. *La Casa que Abraza el Cielo.*

Several niches adorn the perimeter walls of this home (*casa*), and no two are alike! A *talavera*-tiled panel (*tablero*) is surrounded by a frescoed border, above the outdoor bar. The floral motif in the border shows inspiration from the panel and the *talavera* jar at the far right. *La Casa que Abraza el Cielo.*

A *cantera* depiction of Saint Francis is found in another *nicho*. *La Casa que Abraza el Cielo.*

In a corridor, two niches display prized danced masks (*mascaras*). *Casa de la Cuesta.*

Tile was attractively used to enhance this back porch (*portal*) niche. The *corona* at its base is pre-cast concrete. *Casa del Sol y Luna*.

Combinations of mustard (*mostaza*) and cobalt blue tiles were used to coordinate this niche with the colors of the post pedestals and front door surround. *Casa del Sol y Luna*.

Opposite page:
This decorative niche contains a wonderfully carved wooden mermaid (*sirena*) suspended from the back wall, and three fern-filled *talavera* flower pots (*macetas*). *Casa Heyne*.

A two-sided, distressed tin panel, in a Moorish design, is placed into a niche at a stair landing. *Casa Heyne*.

A utilitarain mop basin, outside the kitchen, has become a work of art in this Mexican home. The niche is decorated with random, patterned *talavera* tiles and a carved shell crest. *Casa Heyne*.

Chapter 10.
Fireplaces- *Chimeneas*

Fireplaces provide enumerable opportunities for decorative expression. Not only the selection of an appropriate architectural style and shape, but also the finishing details are limitless. Decorative effects may be achieved with *cantera* stone, *talavera* tile, elaborate faux painting, or painted stucco. Many owners combine several treatments to produce a fireplace that is useful, beautiful, and a focal point in its setting.

The main heat source for this Mexican home (*casa*) is eight interior fireplaces. Not only is each fireplace (*chimenea*) different from the next, but each has a unique, custom-made fire screen. In this corner fireplace, a single row of *talavera* tile surrounds the firebox opening and the brick hearth is raised well above floor level. The wrought iron fire screen is an interesting maze of scrollwork. Comfortable pigskin (*equipale*) chairs are an invitation to relax. *Casa Heyne.*

Talavera tile trims a corner fireplace, running across both the mantle facing and the raised brick hearth. In the center of the iron fire screen, a deer stands among scrolling vines and flowers. *Casa Heyne.*

Unexpected, and utterly delightful, this corner fireplace, in Moorish-style, has an *ojival* arch. After it was painted, Polly Stark Ortega applied a metallic wash. The wrought iron screen follows the shape of the firebox perfectly. *Casa Heyne.*

This fireplace combines the *cantera* stone fireplace surround, carved by Antonio Trenado Flores, with a herringbone-patterned brick in an unusual and attractive manner. The fire screen echoes the details of the surround's carving. *Casa Heyne*.

A extremely tall (fourteen feet high) *cantera* stone fireplace, carved by stonemason Antonio Trenado Flores, anchors one end of the living room. Phoenix birds, flanking the firebox, and a two-headed eagle, cresting the top, are beautifully portrayed. The fireplace was carved in several sections and installed on site. The top of the iron fire screen harmonizes with the surround. *Casa Heyne*.

This bedroom is devoted to religious arts. Here Antonio Trenado Flores respectfully carved Saint Jude, patron saint of lost causes, and Saint Francis, patron saint of animals, on opposing sides of the *cantera* stone fireplace. Close inspection also reveals crosses in the iron screen. *Casa Heyne*.

The outdoor fireplace, located just behind the living room, has a huge carved *cantera* stone mantle with supports carved by Antonio Trenado Flores. A pair of archangels play a horn and a lyre. Cut wood is kept close at the sides, ready to burn. *Casa Heyne.*

A unique outdoor fireplace has been transformed into a work of art. Artist Frank Franklin used a common sight in Mexico for this theme—women making tortillas over an open fire. *La Casa Lomita Linda.*

Blue and white *talavera* tiles surround the firebox opening. The plaster relief above the mantle was created by Kay Steinhilper. Sculptures on the mantle and hearth are by Frank Franklin. *La Casa Lomita Linda.*

During remodeling of the master bedroom, a new fireplace was built into the corner and Frank Franklin was commissioned to adorn it. Besides his decorative painting, he inlaid his stone-carved Indian at the center, as a focal point. The carved and painted blanket box and the painting above it are more of Franklin's work. *La Casa Lomita Linda.*

The corner of this home office has another fireplace hand-painted by artist Frank Franklin. Inspiration for this mural was the arrival of Columbus to the Americas. *La Casa Lomita Linda.*

The master bedroom's corner fireplace has *talavera* tile across the plastered ledge and on top of the hearth. The painting to the left is by José Maria de Servin. *Casa del Sol y Luna.*

In the Great room, the faux finish on this corner fireplace results from mixing yellow and gold paint together. Different bird tiles adorn the ledge that holds a collection of vintage burnished vases from Tonalá. The wrought iron fire screen was found in San Miguel de Allende. *Casa del Sol y Luna*.

Carved *cantera* stone surrounds this fireplace that warms an outdoor living room (*sala*). Oaxacan pierced clay lamps cast romantic shadows on the walls and the African art piece on the mantle as well. A large, old, clay pot from Guerrero is on the left. *Casa de la Condessa*.

The master bedroom's corner fireplace is a wonderful example of creating two visually contrasting patterns with the same tile—the *medio-pañuelo* patterned tile. The surround has been set in a diamond design and the hearth's facing was laid in a herringbone pattern. One tile—two different looks! *Casa de la Condessa*.

Plaster friezes add beautiful decoration to this corner fireplace. Amusing Mexican folk toys parade across the brick trim of the mantle. *Villa Scorpio al Puente.*

A *cantera* stone mantle and hearth decorate this cement corner fireplace. The painting on the right is signed Oscar, and two paintings on the left are by Rhea Gary. A beautifully carved Saint Michael figure is on the mantle. *Estrella de la Mañana.*

Simple and elegant, the *cantera* stone fireplace anchors one end of the courtyard living room (*sala*). A pair of Puebla *talavera* jars is displayed prominently on the mantle. *Estrella de la Mañana.*

A pair of *cantera* stone monkeys (*changuitos*) playing musical instruments support the mantle of this fireplace. *Casa de los Perros*.

A roaring fire beckons from this traditional fireplace. Mustard colored paint is an ideal canvas for the *talavera* tile surrounding the opening. *Casa de los Perros*.

A *medio-pañuelo talavera* tile created this bold geometric herringbone pattern surrounding the fireplace. A pair of *talavera* jars, also in a herringbone motif, stand on the Saltillo flooring. The red candles, in graduated sizes on the mantelpiece, cast romantic shadows. *Red Thunder Ranch*.

Intriguing screens, such as this one, add to the ambiance of a fireplace. This one, crafted by The Village Blacksmith, carries the ranch's brand—opposing R's separated by a T. *Red Thunder Ranch*.

The raised hearth is distinctive and can provide a warm seat. Two *talavera*-lidded jars by Gorky Gonzalez flank the firebox opening, while a signed painting by Francisco (Frank Franklin) hangs above the mantle. *La Casa que Abraza el Cielo*.

A massive fireplace radiates heat into this huge room. The *cantera* stone carved mantle is decked with votive candles and an old wooden head of a *Cristo*. Painted wall murals, on both sides, have been reproduced from 1930s Tlaquepaque pottery motifs. *Casa de Roberts*.

An inviting outdoor fireplace has a wrought iron tree decoration. In spring and summer, when the wood bin is not in use, colorful flower-filled ceramic pots occupy the space. Pigskin (*equipale*) chairs provide comfortable seating. *Casa de Moser*.

Warming the outdoor corridor, this is one of the seven fireplaces around this home that were uniquely hand formed by Antonio Lopez. The surround and mantle are made of concrete and painted in contrasting colors, which serve to intensify the lively effect. The cobalt blue *talavera* jars on the mantle are particularly distinct against pink (*rosa*) walls. *Casa de la Cuesta.*

Right:
Another cement fireplace by Antonio Lopez that utilizes three shades of blue paint for a stunning result. When the draw of air didn't function properly in the fireplace, Lopez added the small arched piece to the front of the firebox and subsequently eliminated the problem. Clay female skeletons (*catrinas*) adorn the mantle. *Casa de la Cuesta.*

Opposite page:
So as not to compete for attention, the fireplace is the same color as the walls in the room, but a contrasting paint color highlights the mantle. The raised hearth is at a comfortable sitting height. *Casa de Wachs.*

Tucked into a corner of the breakfast room and painted the same color as the walls, a small fireplace with raised hearth provides warmth. The built-in bench (*banco*), alongside, is a cozy place for reading or chatting with the cook. *Casa de Wachs*

Below:
The mahogany mantelpiece provides elegance to this fireplace in the corner of the Great room. A folding iron fire screen and pair of carved and painted candlesticks are the only décor used. *Casa de Wachs.*

Chapter 11.
Lighting- *Iluminación*

A multitude of appropriate lighting fixtures awaits the Mexican-style homeowner. Wall sconces, chandeliers, hanging fixtures, and table lamps are readily available in iron, tin, brass, and even *talavera*. Don't overlook an old Mexican clay pot or vase that can be electrified. Owners can use a variety of forms and materials for their lighting.

A shaded, six-light, iron chandelier hanging in the center of the kitchen (*cocina*). *Estrella de la Mañana*.

Opposite page:
A twelve-light, tin chandelier hangs below a hand-painted ceiling treatment. *Casa de Wachs*.

An iron and wood twelve-light chandelier. *Casa Chorro*.

In the *Moroca* bedroom, a pair of punched tin, hanging lanterns, with a faux-brass finish, hang near the bed. *Casa Heyne*.

A turn-of-the century, Rio Grande blanket provides a nice backdrop to the delicate wrought iron chandelier hanging in an interior stairway. *La Casa que Abraza el Cielo.*

Custom-made metal lanterns illuminate an outdoor living room (*sala*). *La Casa Lomita Linda*.

This hanging, pierced iron lantern emits captivating shadows on the interior stairway wall. *Estrella de la Mañana*.

A triple-tiered tin lantern, reminiscent of old processional lanterns, is mounted on a wrought iron bracket (*ménsula)*. The owners have used the same lantern cleverly mounted three different ways, see the next two examples. *Casa Heyne*.

This tin lantern, with brass-colored finish, is mounted as a sconce. *Casa Heyne.*

The same tin lantern as that preceding, but this one mounted to hang downward. *Casa Heyne.*

Hand me a light, please. One of a pair of carved wooden wall sconces. *Estrella de la Mañana*.

An iron bracket group, with electrified candles, lights an interior hallway. *La Casa que Abraza el Cielo*.

An interior, iron, double candleholder rests on an arm bracket. *La Casa que Abraza el Cielo*.

An interior, three-light, iron wall sconce. *Casa de Moser*.

A variation of the preceding fixture. *Casa de Moser*.

148

Interior iron candleholders can be placed anywhere in a home without worrying about adding electrical wiring. The scrolling, black, wrought iron bracket makes a bold statement against a wall of contrasting color. *El Castillo*.

Opposite page:
A shaded, double, iron sconce lights a room from over the fireplace. *Casa de Wachs*.

This tin wall sconce casts beams of directed light. *Casa Heyne*.

A punched tin sconce with quarter moons and star-shaped designs. Tin wears well outside, with an occasional light coat of linseed oil. *Casa de la Cuesta*.

A Mexican, punched tin sconce. *Casa de Wachs*.

A wall-mounted, exterior lantern. *La Casa que Abraza el Cielo*.

This Mexican tin fixture houses a row of lights. *Casa de Moser*.

Twisted iron crowns this exterior, iron, wall sconce. *La Flor del Desierto.*

Iron wall sconces are secured to the rock walls lining a driveway. *Casa Heyne.*

Flat back, exterior, wall sconce. *Casa de Moser.*

A nicely hand wrought, iron lantern on a bracket. *Casa de Ghinis*.

One of the pair of iron lanterns flanking a front gate. *Casa de Moser*.

A lovely *talavera* wall sconce. *La Casa que Abraza el Cielo*.

An iron coach lantern lights this entry. *Casa del Sol y Luna.*

An exterior wall mounted iron coach lantern. *El Castillo*.

Chapter 12.
Arts- *Artes*

No Mexican-style home would be complete without art. An owners' personal taste dictates this finishing touch, whether old or new fine art or folk art. Besides Mexican-made arts, American folk art and Native American art look equally well in these homes

Right:
Mexico's artisans have always been geniuses at using recycled materials. The two street band musicians (*mariachis)* were created from old oil drums. They stand just over six feet tall and were found in Nogales, Sonora. *Casa de Alegret.*

Below:
A charming trio of copper street musicians (*mariachis)*, made in Guadalajara and found in Nogales, appear to serenade swimmers by day and night. The tile mural at the left is from Puebla (circa 1910-'20s), and is signed by the artist, Pedro Sanchez. *Casa del Sol y Luna.*

Opposite page:
An eighteenth-century, English bracket displays a contemporary female skeleton (*catrina)*, by an artist in Queretaro who is fabricating a male counterpart for the owner. *Casa de los Perros.*

Swaying with the wind, this whimsical, three-dimensional, metal angel, sculpted by Frank Franklin, flies freely over a garden. *La Casa Lomita Linda.*

Hours spent scouring antique shops has yielded the collection of painted, hand carved saint figures (*santos*) lining a Moroccan shelf. *Casa de los Perros*.

A large, carved wood Don Quixote figure appears to rest after one of his many adventures before he contemplates his next escapade. *Casa Poco a Poco*.

An unforgettable, eighteenth-century Virgin of *Purisima Concepcion* poses gracefully in this living room (*sala*). At one time, she undoubtedly wore painted clothing, but it has not survived. *Casa Chorro*.

Below:
This lovely mermaid was found in Mexico. *Casa de Ghinis*.

A carved wooden Saint Francis figure seems at home among bougainvillea and palms. *La Casa Lomita Linda*.

Grouping like-items together has always been a good decorating idea. These danced masks (*mascaras*) are clustered together in a niche. The contrasting paint colors work beautifully together and serve to further enhance the magnificent collection. *Casa de la Cuesta*.

Another impressive collection of hand-carved Mexican dance masks. These wooden jewels totally envelop the stone wall in the living room. *Casa de Roberts*.

A whimsical collection of delightfully painted coconut masks fill the home's bar (*cantina*) walls. *Casa de Moser*.

A wooden rendition of *Jesus Cristo* graces a hallway wall. *La Casa que Abraza el Cielo.*

Received as a housewarming gift from a friend, this antique wooden sculpture depicts *Santiago Matamoras.* (Nice *amigo*)! *Casa de Robinson.*

A wall is hung with old Mexican tin religious paintings (*retablos*) in the living room. The owner began collecting these long before it was popular to do so. *Casa de Anonymous.*

A closer look at one of the paintings. *Casa de Anonymous.*

Opposite page:
Religious photographs and prints, framed in old tin niches, capture an important aspect of Mexican culture. *Estrella de la Mañana.*

Right:
Four artists from the *talavera)* pottery workshop, *Talavera de Santa Rosa.* From right to left: Beatriz Angélica Jaramillo Villalobos, Rosa Angélica Hernández, Maria Cruz Aguilar González, and José Ramírez Martínez.

Trees-of-life crowd the window sills of this sun room, while wooden pigs from Guadalajara traipse across the painted concrete floors. *Casa de Anonymous.*

An old Mexican cupboard, found in Nuevo Laredo, is the perfect display piece for an array of vintage pottery. The majority of pieces date from the 1930s from Tlaquepaque, and an impressive Candelario Medrano piece is displayed at the far left. San Antonio, Texas, artist Lisa Mellinger created the hand-painted frescoes by copying Tlaquepaque pottery designs. *Casa de Roberts*.

The owner of this Mexican folk art collection hopes to acquire one of each type of folk art that is made by Mexico's artisans. Here, vintage Tlaquepaque pottery fills the open cupboard (*trastero*) and a clay panel of tiles (*tablero)* hangs below bas-relief woodcarvings. Balancing on the left side are clay versions of bas-relief carvings. *Casa de Anonymous*.

This new panel of tiles (*tablero)* is a faithful adaptation of an old design still in a wall at Puebla. *Casa del Sol y Luna.*

Borrowing design elements from the tiles, Polly Stark Ortega, an artist from San Miguel, painted the frieze around the *talavera* tile panel. *Casa Heyne.*

The little bird (*pajarito*) is the focal point of this *talavera* table made in Delores Hidalgo, Guanajuato, that dates from circa 1950-1960s. It is signed with the initials CB. *La Casa que Abraza el Cielo.*

San Jose Potteries of San Antonio, Texas, produced this tile table in the 1940s. There are twelve pictorial tiles, interspersed throughout the field, portraying delightful Mexican types (*tipos Mexicanos*). *Casa del Sol y Luna.*

Both *talavera* tiles and their borders are the work of Puebla's Uriarte, circa 1930s. *Casa del Sol y Luna.*

Found in Puebla, the *talavera* tile panel (*tablero*) is the work of Pedro Sanchez, circa 1900s. *Casa del Sol y Luna.*

A magnificent eleven-by-fourteen-foot mural covers the southern facade of a house in one of Tucson's barrio districts. It is signed Francisco (Frank Franklin) and dated 1990.The placard under the automobile reads as follows:

> *Esta es mi vida* (This is my life*)*
> *Este es mi amor* (This is my love)
> *Que pasa mi vida tranquila* (My life passes calmly)
> *Sin tristesa* (Without sadness)
> *Y sin dolor* (And without pain)
> *Y el día que me muera* (And the day that I die)
> *Y que dios me lleva de aquí* (And God takes me from here)
> *Voy a segur pintado para nunca olvidar me de ti.* (I will go, leaving
>   a painting for you to remember me by.)

Casa de Baugh.

Traditional art coexists with modern art in the pool courtyard. The sculpture was created by Tucson artist Steven Derks, and the mural was painted by Frank Franklin. *La Casa Lomita Linda*.

Found in Michoacán, the sun and moon motif carved flowerpot (*maceta*) rests temporarily on an old, San Antonio, cement tile table and will be hung from one of the beams. *Casa del Sol y Luna.*

A bas-relief carved planter box, in a floral motif, dangles from iron chains at this front entrance. Notice a tile mural embedded into the plastered wall. *Casa de Ghinis.*

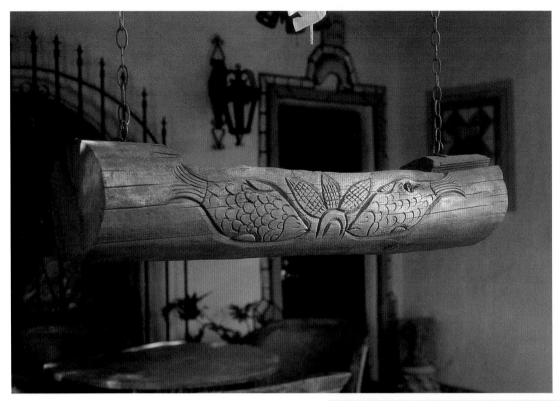

Michoacán is well known for its variety of wood carving and this fish motif planter box is a fine example. *Talavera* tile borders the front door. *Casa de Ghinis.*

Under the protection of the porch (*portal*), brightly colored Mexican fabric pillows, matching the painted nine-paneled screen, create a pleasing combination. *La Flor del Desierto.*

Opposite page:
The painting and the carved and painted trunk (*baúl*) are the work of Frank Franklin. *La Casa Lomita Linda.*

An antique, oil-on-canvas rendition of San Nicholas Tolentino brightens this room. *Casa de Black*.

A Mexican kitchen (*cocina*) would not be complete without its own version of San Pascual Bailón, the patron saint of the kitchen. This work was commissioned by the owner from Gonzalo E. *La Casa que Abraza el Cielo*.

This charming, unsigned, Mexican folk portrait, in the style of Horacio and Labios, hangs in a kitchen under a carved display shelf. *La Casa que Abraza el Cielo*.

A painted trunk (*baúl*) from Olinalá rests below a fine Mexican religious painting (*retablo*) in the hallway. Mexican dance masks frame the doorway through which a collection of vintage Mexican game boards is visible. *Casa de Anonymous*.

A Mexican, oil on canvas painting, in its original frame, is signed by Agapito Labios, circa 1940s. *Casa del Sol y Luna.*

Above and right:
Three contemporary paintings from Michoacán, in the *costumbrista* style decorate a hallway wall. *La Flor del Desierto.*

A five-foot-wide hallway affords space for a gallery of over thirty vintage bas-relief wood panels. *Casa del Sol y Luna.*

The bench (*banco*) is a superb example of Mexican tin craftsmanship. *Casa de Wachs.*

Under the protection of the porch (*portal*), a painted and tiled, two-door cupboard provides storage and bright decoration. An unusual aspect of the design is the use of *talavera* dinner plates, recessed in the door panels. *Casa de la Cuesta.*

A colonial-blue painted cabinet (*armario*) stands between two doorways and showcases an early Gorky Gonzalez *talavera* pot and a pair of Guerrero-style glazed clay figures. *Casa de los Perros*.

Found in Guatemala, this fine carved and painted cupboard has a sun and moon motif. Guatemalan figures of saints (*Santos*) surround and protect the cupboard. Wall paint: Dunn-Edwards® Pure Butter. *Casa de Franklin*.

An exquisitely painted table and chairs from Michocán (*Costumbrista* style) has finely painted details. It provides an enticing place for a traditional game of checkers. *Casa de Wachs*.

A closer look at one of the painted chairs. *Casa de Wachs*.

Appendix 1.
Tile Illustration- *Medio-pañuelo*

Medio-pañuelo *Talavera* Tile

 Medio-pañuelo means half-handkerchief. In this instance, we refer to a *talavera* tile with an imaginary line at a 45° angle, with a contrasting color or design on each half of the angle. It offers several different installation methods as evidenced throughout the *casas* in both books.

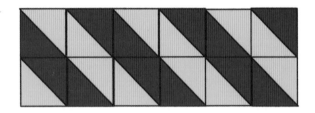 **Angled Stripe**

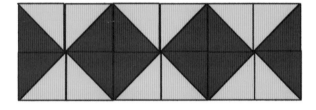 **Diamond**

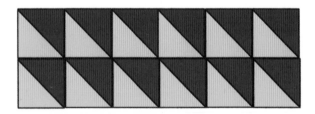 **Eclipsing Squares**

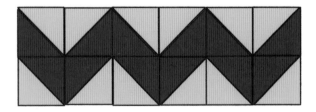 **Herringbone**

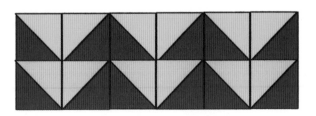 **Sawtooth**

Appendix 2.
Paint Sample Illustrations

The following eleven paint sample cards were graciously supplied by Dunn-Edwards Paints® and are used with permission. Dunn-Edwards® is a registered trademark of Dunn-Edwards Corporation.

Crimson

Mayan

Rio Fleece

Fenbrook

T.J. Water

Pure Butter

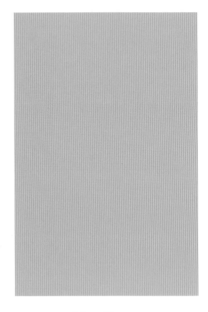

Vice Versa

Swiss Coffee

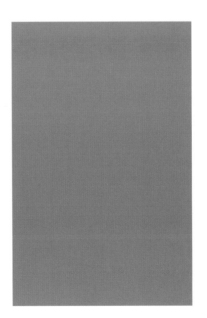

Butter Up

Bristol

Wineberry

The following three paint sample cards were graciously supplied by Benjamin Moore & Co. and are used with permission.

063

308

1364

Glossary

Agua. Water
Alacena. A cupboard in the wall
A la derecha. To the right
Alberca. Pool
Amigo. Friend
Arboles de la vida. Trees of life
Arcada. Arcade or row of arches
Arista. Salient angle
Armario. Cabinet
Arquitecto. Architect
Artes. Arts
Asador. Barbeque grill
Azul. Blue
Azulejo. Glazed tile

Balaustrada. Balustrade
Banco. Bench
Bandidos. Bandits
Baño. Bathroom
Barandales. Underpieces of a balustrade
Barras. Bars or rods
Batea. Painted tray
Baúl. Trunk
Bienvenido. Welcome
Bóveda. Arch or vault
Brasero. Cooking center, usually of masonry with gas or charcoal

Canales. Gutters projecting from roof
Canción. Song
Cantera. Quarry stone
Cantina. Bar
Cariño. Love or affection
Cartas. Letters
Casa. House
Cascada. Waterfall
Casita. Small house
Catrina. Female skeleton

Changuito. Small monkey
Chimenea. Fireplace
Citarilla. Open fence or balustrade usually built of brick or tile
Clavo. Nail or iron spike
Cobalto. Cobalt
Cochera. Garage
Cocina. Kitchen
Columna. Column
Comedor. Dining room
Concha. Shell
Cornisa. Cornice
Corona. Crown (also the name of a Mexican brand of beer)
Corredor. Corridor
Costumbrista. A type of art being produced in Michoacán
Cristo. Chirst, image of Christ crucified
Cúpula. Cupola
Cuña. A light weight brick used for bóveda ceilings

Danos el pan nuestro de cada día. Give us our daily bread
Desayunador. Breakfast room

Elegante. Elegant
Entrada. Entry
Equipale. Pigskin furniture
Escalera. Stairway
Espadaña. Section of a wall crowning the facade with arched openings
Estrella. Star
Exvoto. Painting offering thanks

Fachada exterior. Front facade
Fachada frontal. Front facade
Fachada posterior. Rear facade
Flores. Flowers
Fuente. Fountain

Herradura. Horseshoe shape
Hierro. Iron
Hombre. Man
Huéspedes. Guests

Iglesia. Church
Iluminación. Lighting

Jardín. Garden
Jarrones. Large jars
Laja. A thin flat stone, lava rock
Llamador. Door knocker
Luna. Moon

Maceta. Flowerpot
Maestro. Master craftsman
Mariachi. Mexican street band
Máscara. Mask
Medio-pañuelo. Half-handkerchief pattern
Ménsula. Bracket
Moldura de arco. Arch trim or molding
Mostaza. Mustard
Música. Music

Nicho. Niche

Ojival. A type of arch used in Moorish designs
Ojo de buey. Ox eye

Padre. Father
Pajarito. Little bird
Pecho de paloma. Breast of dove
Perro. Dog
Pescado. Fish
Petatillo. A type of thin brick used for pathways and roofs
Pilar(es). Pillar(s)
Portal(es). Porch(s)
Pórtico. Covered porch, usually at the entry
Postigo. Small door usually inside another door

Portón. Gate
Principal. Main
Puerta. Door

Recámara. Bedroom
Reja. Iron grating or railing, usually in front of a door or window
Repisa. Hanging open shelf
Retablo. Religious painting
Rosa. Pink

Sala. Living room
San. Contraction for Saint
Santo. Saint
Sapo. Frog
Silla. Chair
Sillón. Couch
Sirena. Mermaid
Sol. Sun

Tablero. Panel of tiles, usually comprising a mural
Talavera. Hand-painted, twice-fired, tin-glazed earthenware
Taller. Workshop
Techo. Ceiling
Teja. Clay roof tile
Tipos Mexicanos. Mexican types
Torre. Tower or turret
Tortuga. Turtle
Trastero. Open cupboard
Tristeza. Sadness

Vestíbulo. Vestibule
Viga. Beam

Y. And

Zaguán. Passageway from street to inner courtyard
Zoclo. Baseboard

Bibliography

Garrison, G. Richard and George W. Rustay. *Mexican Houses: A Book of Photographs & Measured Drawings:* New York: Architectural Book Publishing Co., Inc., 1930.

Grizzard, Mary. *Spanish Colonial Art and Architecture of Mexico and the U.S. Southwest.* Lanham: University Press of America, Inc., 1986.

Newcomb, Rexford. *The Spanish House for America: Its Design, Furnishing, and Garden.* Philadelphia: J. B. Lippincott Company, 1927.

O'Gorman, Patricia W. *Patios and Gardens of Mexico.* Stamford: Architectural Book Publishing Co., Inc., 1979.

El patio de mi casa: portadas, portones, zaguanes y patios de la habitación mexicana. Mexico: Instituto del Fondo Nacional de la Vivienda para los Trabajadores, 1990.

Sexton, R.W. *Spanish Influence on American Architecture and Decoration.* New York: Brentano's, 1927.

Shipway, Verna Cook and Warren Shipway. *Decorative Design in Mexican Homes.* New York: Architectural Book Publishing Co., Inc., 1966.

—. *Houses of Mexico: Origins and Traditions.* New York: Architectural Book Publishing Co., Inc., 1970.

—. *Mexican Homes of Today.* New York: Architectural Book Publishing Co., Inc., 1964.

—. *The Mexican House: Old & New.* 1960. Reprint, New York: Architectural Book Publishing Co., Inc., 1963.

—. *Mexican Interiors.* 1962. Reprint, Stamford: Architectural Book Publishing Co., Inc., 1988.

Yañez, Enrique. *18 Residencias de Arquitectos Mexicanos: 18 Homes of Mexican Architects:.* Mexico: Ediciones Mexicanas S.A., 1951.